*Affectionately,*
*T. S. Eliot*

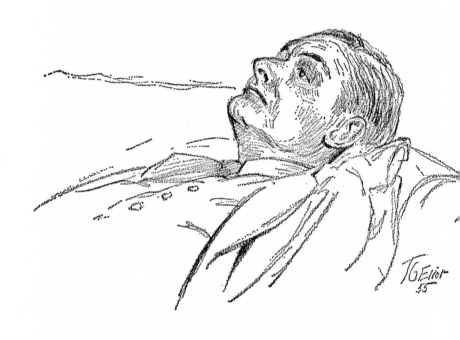

*T. S. Eliot*
*Pencil and Chalk Drawing*
*from life*
*by his sister-in-law*
*Theresa G. Eliot, 1955*
*(See page 83.)*

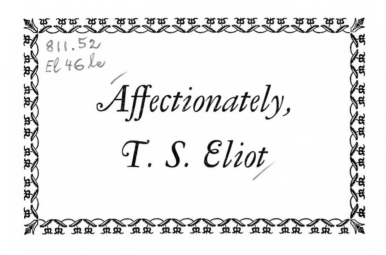

# Affectionately, T. S. Eliot

## The Story of a Friendship: 1947-1965

by

## William Turner Levy

and

## Victor Scherle

J. B. LIPPINCOTT COMPANY
*Philadelphia and New York*

The letters written by T. S. Eliot are copyright © 1968 by Mrs. T. S. Eliot.

The quotations from *Four Quartets* by T. S. Eliot are made by the kind permission of Harcourt, Brace & World, Inc. The quotation on pages 14-15 is
from "Little Gidding"; on page 41 is from "Little Gidding"; on page 115
is from "Little Gidding"; on page 121 is from "The Dry Salvages"; on page
125 is from "The Dry Salvages"; on page 128 is from "Little Gidding."

*Book design by Joe Crossen*

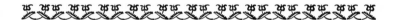

*To Fannie Hurst*

*With a deep sense of appreciation for her friendship*

## Preface

T. S. Eliot was fifty-nine years of age, and I was twenty-five, when the first letters passed between us. Our friendship was uninterrupted for the next eighteen years. If Eliot were alive today, he would this year be celebrating his eightieth birthday.

My friend Mr. Victor Scherle saw that there was a narrative here, one which made clear how good and generous a man Eliot was. Together, as we wrote, we turned to my letters from Eliot, more than seventy in all, and to my notes made at the time of each of our meetings. Mr. Scherle asked endless questions, evaluated and shaped a plethora of material, and summoned from the recesses of my memory details I had not thought of for years.

"Praise," writes Sir Thomas Browne, "is a debt we owe unto the virtue of others." That this tribute appears is due to the skill and diligence of Victor Scherle, and to the graciousness of Valerie Eliot, by whose permission her husband's letters are quoted.

WILLIAM TURNER LEVY

*Pine Knob Cabin*
*Roaring Branch Camps*
*Arlington, Vermont*
*February, 1968*

[7]

# Chapter One

One afternoon during the Blitz, I walked across Russell Square to the offices of Faber & Faber. It was 1944, I was twenty-two years old and stationed with the United States Army in England. On that particular day—it was during a week's furlough in London—I had visited the Poets' Corner in Westminster Abbey for the first time. After a frugal lunch at Samuel Johnson's Cheshire Cheese, I was in a perfect frame of mind to take Padraic Colum's advice and call on T. S. Eliot.

Having majored in English at both City College and Columbia University in New York, I knew two men who were friends of Eliot—Padraic Colum and Mark Van Doren. In both cases, their paths had crossed Eliot's from time to time and they all retained that sort of casual contact with each other that is common between men of letters.

Eliot wasn't in at the publishing house of which he was a director, so I left a note indicating that I was a friend of

Padraic Colum, who had suggested that I call on him and introduce myself without the formality of an appointment.

I was not to see Eliot until three years later, when, in 1947, he stood on the platform of the auditorium in the Frick Collection in New York to read his recantation on Milton. It was an invitational affair to which I had been invited by the director of the Frick Collection—the poet Frederick Mortimer Clapp.

I had written Eliot in advance saying that I would be present on that date and reminded him that I had called at his office in London during the war. After the lecture, I hoped to meet him, but once again I was disappointed, for he was whisked away to a small private reception to which I had not been invited. A few days later I received my first letter from Eliot, dated May 15, 1947, in which he said that he was "extremely sorry" to have missed seeing me, adding "I hope and believe that we shall succeed in meeting on your next visit in 1948" when, as I had written him, I would be in London gathering material for my doctoral dissertation on William Barnes, the Dorset poet. Eliot suggested that I write to him again after his return to London so that he would "be able to reply I hope at more length and greater leisure."

I did write, enclosing a photograph of myself along with autobiographical facts. In the months that followed, I sent him newspaper clippings about himself, a brief note, and several greeting cards, but in all cases asked that he not trouble to reply.

In July of 1948 I reached England aboard the Cunard liner *Media*. Arriving in London, I immediately telephoned Eliot's office and through his secretary was invited for tea on Monday, July 26.

As the taxi wound its way from Onslow Square, where I was staying, to Russell Square, I became more and more nervous. On my lap I had my briefcase containing a first edition of *The Family Reunion,* which I hoped Eliot would inscribe, and next to me on the seat, a present for Eliot—two large cans of American mints! I knew that candy was a luxury in Britain, not easily available owing to postwar food shortages.

At Faber & Faber, after stating my business to the receptionist, I was asked to make myself comfortable in a small waiting room. For ten minutes I looked out at the Square, too anxious to sit down. Then a matronly lady entered and said, "Mr. Eliot will see you now." I followed her into a nearby elevator which she operated herself and, when we had reached the desired floor, down a narrow corridor to an unmarked door which she knocked at twice and then immediately opened. I entered.

The window was directly behind Eliot, and I could only see his rising silhouette. I was immediately impressed with his size. The tall, heavy-set man, slightly stooped, moved slowly and gracefully toward me, offering a large hand in welcome.

"I recognize you from the photograph you sent. I'm very glad you could come." His voice was deeply resonant and the pattern of his speech deliberate. As I took his hand I saw that his brow was furrowed, but he was smiling pleasantly, if quizzically. His dress was conventional and conservative. He wore a thin-striped dark gray suit, a white shirt and a dark gray checkered tie, but his jacket was unbuttoned and his white breast-pocket handkerchief was noticeably rumpled.

He escorted me to a chair across from his own. There were only two chairs in the room, which was almost monastic in its simplicity and bareness; it was, however, perfectly equipped to serve as the workroom of a writer-publisher. Before I sat down I gave him my gift of mints, which he thanked me for and then placed next to him on his desk.

I started to apologize for having written him so many letters and notes, but he stopped me, raising his right hand slightly and saying, "I was very pleased with your letters, but you will have to understand that I seldom have the time to answer, although I am always glad to hear from you."

A tea tray was brought in and placed on a small table between us.

"You will have to excuse office tea and make the best of it," Eliot said while pouring. On the tray there were cigarettes and half a dozen biscuits.

We talked about my work on the Barnes book, about Robinson Jeffers and his poems on Ireland, about Columbia and City College, about the Van Dorens and the Colums. Then Eliot said, "You have some questions for me—fire away. I remember some of them from your excellent letters, and I am much interested."

The questions I wished to ask Eliot concerned his work, particularly his play *The Family Reunion,* about which he commented: "I am very fond of some of the poetry in it, but with the passage of time I have come to think it a failure as a play."

Offering me a third cup of tea, Eliot said, "It's awful tea; don't take it to be polite." I accepted the tea because it was warm and sweet, although it was lacking in flavor.

"Now, may I ask *you* a question?" Eliot continued with a slight grin. I could tell by the playful look in his eyes that it was not going to be a serious question.

[*12*]

I told him that I had no objection.

"What does the phrase 'harefoot over the moon' mean in *The Family Reunion?*"

"Nothing," I told him, without a moment's hesitation.

"That's right," he answered laughing, "if I were a better poet I'd have cut it out. But I liked it!"

More than an hour passed and I felt that I might be overstaying. But when I offered to leave, Eliot said, "Do you have to be somewhere?"

I told him "No," so we continued talking. I mentioned that I liked London, particularly because it was quiet compared to New York. Eliot said, "London is almost as bad as New York now. All modern cities are impossibly crowded. For me, one of the pleasures of a city is being able to walk, and stop and look down streets at buildings, in shop windows, across parks. But, now, you get in the way if you pause."

He asked me how I liked teaching at City College, and the ensuing conversation led him to reminisce about his own early experience teaching youngsters. He said, "I suppose what I liked least about teaching was marking papers. Perhaps because they weren't very good papers, proving, no doubt, that I wasn't a very good teacher!"

Before I left, Eliot offered to give me a copy of *The Family Reunion*. He searched his revolving bookstand for one and found a reprint. When I showed him my first edition, he seemed genuinely perplexed: "I would prefer to give you a copy of the play myself, but I am forced to admit that it is more important for you to have the first edition." He inscribed it slowly, carefully curling each word onto the page.

"I'm going to America in September, and I'll come to see you in New York," Eliot told me.

I said that if it would be more convenient I could come to Princeton, where I knew he would be working at the Institute for Advanced Study.

Eliot was looking at the two cans of mints I had brought. Now he looked up at me, raised both eyebrows, smiled and replied, "I'm glad you said that. Yes, it would be. When I'm in New York it's for more than one engagement and we'd be rushed. Yes, do come. I'll write you when I get settled. If you don't hear from me by the fifteenth of October, you write and remind me."

Eliot's eyes once again returned to the mints, and he said, not looking at me, "Thank you again for the present. I will take them home the first night I'm going straight home . . . there are so many. Thank you."

In the course of our conversation I had mentioned how impressed I was with the dignity and reserve of both Russell Square and the building of Faber & Faber. Eliot responded by telling me that during the war he had been a fire watcher stationed on the roof of Faber & Faber: "We had to watch the fires and report them as quickly as they occurred. You will be interested to know that the lines from 'Little Gidding' came out of this experience."

He then recited his own words from that poem, which is the last of the *Four Quartets*:

> *"Ash on an old man's sleeve*
> *Is all the ash the burnt roses leave.*
> *Dust in the air suspended*
> *Marks the place where a story ended.*
> *Dust inbreathed was a house—*
> *The wall, the wainscot and the mouse.*

*The death of hope and despair,*
*This is the death of air."*

For the first time I heard the poet speak his own verse, and I was deeply moved.

"You see," Eliot remembered, "during the Blitz the accumulated debris was suspended in the London air for hours after a bombing. Then it would slowly descend and cover one's sleeves and coat with a fine white ash. I often experienced this effect during long night hours on the roof."

This led me to recount my own eerie experience after I had crossed the Rhine and entered Wesel several days after it had been bombarded. I described to Eliot the almost underwater illusion that the fallout of dust had created. He asked detailed questions and we spoke of the destruction caused by war. I told him that in a Wesel street I found, fallen from the collapsed wall of a house, a small framed print, picturing a castle, and bearing the inscription, in German, "My Home Is My Castle." Eliot cupped his right hand to his chin, said nothing, but slowly shook his head from side to side.

At the door we talked of another result of the war: the hostility of the Russians, and the current conflict over Berlin. Eliot showed serious concern when he said, "We'll have trouble with the Communist world. Berlin is on all our minds now."

We shook hands and he said, "Good-by. Thank you for your letters and for coming. I'll look forward to seeing you."

Out on the street I remembered seeing in Eliot's office, much to my surprise and delight, only two items on his fireplace mantel—a photograph of Virginia Woolf and the Easter card I had sent to him four months before.

[*15*]

# Chapter Two

Immediately after my visit, I sent Eliot a note thanking him for tea at his office, saying, "How pleasant to meet Mr. Eliot!" a play on the opening line of his satirical poem, "Lines for Cuscuscaraway and Mirza Murad Ali Beg."

I returned to New York during the latter part of August and on September 23, when I thought Eliot would soon be arriving at Princeton, I wrote him a welcoming letter addressed to the Institute for Advanced Study, which he acknowledged on October 7, two days after his arrival.

On October 13 he wrote again, saying, "I am only just beginning to be settled but I will write to you when I am sure of a weekend free and suggest your coming down and having lunch with me."

Although originally scheduled to remain at the Institute for several months in order to write a play which became known as *The Cocktail Party,* his stay was cut short by the notification of his having won the 1948 Nobel Prize for Literature.

I telephoned him as soon as I heard the news. "I am," he said, "particularly pleased for the sake of poetry."

I learned from him that the prize carried with it certain annoyances and obligations. "It seems already to be breaking into my privacy," he said, "and now it will be necessary for me to return to London and prepare for the presentation." He added, "It is so beautiful here this time of the year . . . I am sorry you must miss it."

After his return to London, T. S. Eliot and I began a more regular correspondence. In thanking me for a box of Christmas food I had sent, he wrote in February of 1949: "I have to thank you for your generosity in sending a Christmas parcel, which although it arrived some time after Christmas [here Eliot wrote a footnote in longhand, "naturally with the strike"] is none the less appreciable. Apart from the material benefit conferred I particularly appreciate it as a testimony of your generous friendliness."

Two months later, Eliot wrote: "I am going to thank you for your Easter present which touched and surprised me anew —as in any case I should be writing to thank you for your interesting letter of the 5th April. I am glad to have your news and especially about your own activities though sorry to infer that there is no likelihood of your coming over this summer. In that case we are not likely to meet again until next year."

On January 3, 1950, he wrote: "I have several things to thank you for. First, for the most opulent food parcel, full of good things, which arrived during my absence in Germany [on a lecture tour], and further for two very delightful letters and Christmas card. I am always happy to hear from you, though I am myself a poor correspondent. I am now leaving for a six weeks holiday and going to South Africa. You may be assured that I shall not fly, since the chief object is the rest and relaxation of the sea voyage, and I certainly never fly the Atlantic if a steamship is available. I shall hope to see you on my way through New York in October."

In October, Eliot visited the University of Chicago to lecture and give poetry readings, remaining there through November as a poet in residence, at the end of which time he planned before returning to England to spend a few days in New York at the apartment of the artist and illustrator, E. McKnight Kauffer. He wrote me suggesting that I call him there on December 1 to arrange a meeting.

I did so, and the next day at three o'clock in the afternoon, Eliot and I met for the second time. He came to the door of the Kauffer apartment, extended his hand, and said, "William Turner Levy, it is good to see you again!"

He showed me into a large, modern living room which overlooked Central Park and to an enormous chair that looked suspiciously uncomfortable. Eliot sat in a similar chair to my left, sliding a package of cigarettes across the huge glass-topped coffee table that stretched before me. He was wearing a gray-striped worsted suit, a light blue checkered shirt, dark blue checkered silk tie—and there was a white rumpled handkerchief in his breast pocket. In the years I knew him he was never without a similarly displayed handkerchief, which he used not as a decoration, but for the practical purpose of wiping his brow and hands. This habit of his suggested to me an always suitable gift. Over the years I sent him numerous white handkerchiefs bordered with various colors and sometimes initialed. He always considered them a luxury and a pleasure to use.

Eliot said to me, "I am gratified to have a quiet time to sit down with someone I really want to see." He smiled and asked, "Do you want to know what it is like to be famous?" Before I had time to reply, he answered his own question. "I have not known until this last year; now I have a kind of Broadway fame that the newspapers can understand, and all due to the success of *The Cocktail Party* and my winning the Nobel Prize. No one thinks of me as a poet any more, but as a celebrity."

As if to prove his point, the telephone and doorbell rang almost continuously during my visit. Eliot never answered them, but asked me if I minded the noise. He said, "It does not bother me if it does not bother you. Everybody wants you to meet their friends. Huge cocktail parties. No time for talk. The din of its noise in your ears. But tell me about yourself."

I told him that I was working on the Barnes book, deploring my slowness, and said that I lacked the competitive instinct.

"That is delightfully unusual in these times," Eliot replied, "and very good because you arrive on your own and to stay. It is more sure."

Eliot told me that his stay at the University of Chicago had been "wonderful, but very exhausting."

He was smoking as he talked. Occasionally he would look at the cigarette which he held between his thumb and index fingers in a vertical position and then slowly and carefully shift it from one hand to another while continuing to talk just as deliberately. Sometimes his words seemed to be directed to the cigarette.

The room was becoming darker and a light rain was falling outside. The glow of Eliot's cigarette partly illuminated his face as he sat hunched over in a meditative attitude.

He now talked of his recent lectures in Germany. "I met many wonderful individuals, like the Bishop of Hanover. But they were all of the same social class. I didn't have the opportunity to meet people from different walks of life, and although I spoke to large crowds, I didn't make personal contact with the German on the street. Chiefly because I had to move constantly. I had twelve meetings to speak at in six weeks in the American and British zones. War has mutilated the face of Germany, as you know, but some things haven't changed: the beer, for instance, which I like, is as good as ever. Now, may I offer you a drink?" he said, rising and gesturing to a small nearby bar. "I don't think there is any beer here, though."

"Well, in that case I'll take a bourbon and water," I replied.

He made the same drink for himself, although I noticed that his was lighter than mine.

We toasted by clinking glasses together and Eliot said, "Good wishes!" I knew that he meant it.

After he settled back into his chair I asked him if he had known Charles Williams, whose novel *All Hallow's Eve* I had just read.

"I was not intimate with him, although I knew him for a good number of years, informally." Eliot now began tapping the top of the coffee table with his fingertips in time with the rhythm of his speech, emphasizing certain words, never looking up, but totally engrossed in a desire to be precise. "He had strong religious convictions, a profound sense of good and evil, and an urgent desire to communicate their living reality. Unfortunately, he did not have the mastery of a writer. In all of his novels and plays the ideas were imposed upon the characters and caused the manipulation of the plot. Of course, if the reader is disposed to accept his view at the start, there is pleasure to be derived from his work. However, Williams would not be convincing to a reader who had not been conditioned to his premises. I find his poetry difficult and the symbols and meanings difficult, and have never enjoyed its surface enough to look deeper."

Eliot suddenly looked around with a startled expression on his face, rose and lit a lamp. Absorbed in conversation, he had just realized that it had grown quite dark in the room. I quickly glanced at my wrist watch and saw that the time was four-thirty. I had been with Eliot for an hour and a half. Anxious not to impose on his generosity, I immediately put out my cigarette, stood up and said, "You must be very busy now just before having to sail for England tomorrow."

Eliot likewise looked at his wrist watch, but in a manner entirely different from the one I had used. As though considering it a very serious matter, he slowly and methodically raised his left hand and with his right hand carefully pushed back his coat sleeve and shirt sleeve at the same time and then painstakingly at close range, studied the face of the dial. Finally, he seemed to equate the hour and his obligation to it by admitting to me that he was very busy. With a sigh of resignation he added, "I never have enough time. In just a few minutes some people are going to pick me up."

Eliot walked me to the door of the apartment and then out in the hall to the self-service elevator. He said, "Write. I greatly enjoy hearing from you—even though I answer only one letter to your three."

I shook hands with him and then stepped into the waiting,

empty elevator. As I did, Eliot said, "God bless you, son. I will have you in mind." He turned away as the doors closed and the elevator started to descend. Then when he was out of sight I heard him say, "Even in my prayers."

# Chapter Three

Eliot suffered a mild heart attack and was hospitalized shortly after his return to London. Learning of his illness from *The New York Times*, I wrote to him immediately to express my concern. I received the following answer, addressing me for the first time by my first name:

"Thank you for your kind note of March 5th. I am dictating this letter in the Clinic, where I shall be detained for another five or six days. The report that I intend to go to the South, either Spain or Italy, is correct. It is curious how all these things manage to get into the press. I shall await with interest, your report on *Murder in the Cathedral,* and I hope, at the same time, that you will give me more news of yourself."

The mention of *Murder in the Cathedral* referred to an annual student production at Columbia University, where I had just completed my graduate courses toward the doctorate. I had told Eliot that I was going to see the production, which was to be held in the University's St. Paul's Chapel, and that I liked the idea of its being performed in a church.

"I cannot conceive of the play being done on a conventional stage," he later told me. "It is not, after all, a commercial endeavor. I wrote it to be performed in Canterbury Cathedral as a religious celebration, and so I would always prefer that it be performed in a consecrated setting. I do not know why anyone would want to see it as entertainment."

During the year of 1951 I continued to keep Eliot informed of my activities, teaching English at City College, completing my book on Barnes for my doctorate and taking courses at New York's Union Theological Seminary in preparation for my entrance into the Episcopal priesthood. Aside from a Christmas card, I didn't hear from him again until January 16, 1952, at which time he wrote:

"Your kindness and generosity are endless, and far exceed any kindness or service that I have ever had the opportunity to perform for you. The fruit cake and the package of food have both arrived. The former is luxury with the additional distinction of having been baked by yourself, and the latter containing very important articles of food: a remarkable cheese which I have not yet broken into, and some very useful tins of ham and pineapple. Thank you with all my heart.

"I have been, and I fear shall always be owing to my circumstances, a very irregular correspondent, but I wish to assure you once again that your letters are always welcome, and that I follow your activities and your vocation with the greatest interest and the warmest sympathy. I look forward in the hope of a meeting with you when I come to New York in the spring."

In the course of my studies at Union Theological Seminary I met and became a friend of the distinguished theologian Reinhold Niebuhr. When he became seriously ill as the result of a crippling stroke, I wrote to Eliot about it. Eliot had known Niebuhr in the days when the latter was living in England and the two of them belonged to a discussion group called "The Moot." Other members had included Karl Mannheim, the influential sociologist, and William Temple, who was to become the Archbishop of Canterbury.

In answer to my letter about Niebuhr, Eliot wrote on March 4, 1952:

"I had not heard of Dr. Niebuhr's illness. I am not surprised, because it seemed to me that he had been living and working much too hard for many years past. His vitality and energy used to be stupendous, but sometimes, it is these men of immense energy who fail to take notice of the warning signals of middle-age, and do not moderate their activities in time. I am very sorry to hear of this, and hope that you will be able to let me have better news."

The next time I heard from Eliot was when he telephoned me on Saturday evening, the following May 10.

"Hello . . . William . . . this is T. S. Eliot, here. I am pleased to report that I am in New York, not many blocks, really, from you! I wanted to see whether you were engaged tomorrow morning, and if we might slip out and go to Mass somewhere together."

I told him that I would be pleased to go to church with him, but asked if we could go to my own parish, All Angels' Church on West 81st Street. He knew that it was a Low Church and that there would not be a celebration of the Holy

Communion (or Mass) at the eleven o'clock service as there would be in a High Church. (As the Episcopal Church is by its very nature and origin both Catholic and Protestant—being the American equivalent of the Church of England—some parishes are more Catholic in their emphasis, some more Protestant.) He considerately replied, "Yes, yes . . . I like a Morning Prayer once in a while, especially when it is well done, and I would like to go to *your* church."

And so I arranged to pick him up at ten-thirty the next morning.

When I saw him he took my hand in both of his and said, "Well, William, how nice. Ah, we must be on our way!" Upon first meeting, Eliot's deliberateness of speech always surprised me. We made our way to the street and entered a cab I had waiting.

After assuring me that he was in very good health, he asked me about the courses I was teaching that term. I told him in some detail of my work and then he said, "I taught at two boys' schools, as you know, for a year and a half before going to work in a bank as a clerk. I thought the long vacation would provide me with time to read and write, but I found the teaching took so much out of me that I had no desire to work during the vacations." He paused a moment and added, "To hold the classes' attention you must project your personality on them, and some people enjoy doing that; I couldn't, it took too much out of me. You must have a vocation for it." I admitted that I did.

A few years later, I referred to this "vocation" again and delighted him with the story of how Adlai Stevenson, upon being fulsomely introduced as a great orator, opened his speech by remarking, "I can't wait to hear myself speak!"

As the cab negotiated the streets from east to west, Eliot queried me on the intelligence and moral and religious literacy of my students. I explained the highly competitive entrance examinations that provided us with our student body at the tuition-free City College.

"It is one way," he said, "but doesn't it tend to bring together only those who are competitive by instinct, those who are also eager to compete in the world afterwards?" More seriously, he added, "Do they think of learning as an end in itself, or merely as a means to more practical and desirable ends?"

When we arrived at the church, Eliot met my mother and father for the first time. Their remarks both then and after the service were warm and eager: it was obvious that Eliot and my parents liked each other at once.

The service was a disaster! It was ten minutes after eleven when the rector announced that the electric organ was not working, and so the procession of the choir and clergy was reduced to their simply entering the chancel from a side door. All singing was necessarily *a cappella,* except that almost as soon as the opening hymn was begun, the organ, somehow, emitted a loud, screeching note that did not relent until after the sermon was over, about half an hour later. Apparently no one could stop the eerie sound. The junior choir giggled. Parishioners turned to look at one another in consternation. What was meant to be a festival service of thanksgiving for a successful May Fair turned into a depressingly flat occasion. I was appalled when the sermon turned out to be a report on the Fair!

The organist was able to repair the organ eventually, and then played it with a vengeance in a deafeningly grand manner.

At the conclusion of the service, I led Eliot directly across the aisle to meet the rector's wife, who had been alerted that Eliot was coming. She proceeded to introduce each of her three children in turn to "Mr. C. S. Lewis," adding that it was a day they would all remember! I could see that Eliot was vastly amused.

At the main door on the way out, Eliot greeted the rector, saying, "You have a beautiful church, sir. I have been a warden of my own parish for many years and I am used to the fact that minor disruptions of all kinds always seem more important than they are."

One or two of the younger people recognized Eliot because they had been at a public reading he had given at the Y.M.H.A. a night or two before. This was the kind of recognition that pleased him.

"It is nice to meet persons who are interested in your work," he said, after we had said good-by to my parents and entered another cab.

Eliot had only a half hour before he was due back at the apartment where he was staying. I asked him if he'd like to spend it at the Central Park Zoo. He was delighted with what I thought he took to be an unorthodox suggestion.

As I settled back in the cab, I was thankful that I hadn't extended to Eliot the rector's invitation (by telephone the night before) that, as a distinguished layman, he read one of the lessons in the service. I knew that Eliot's regard for privacy and his lack of a meaningful connection with All Angels' Church would be reasons enough for his refusal.

Eliot commented favorably on the large number of young people in the congregation, something he said was not true of English churches. "In England, our ministers cannot deal with the young effectively because they live in the past; they do not even understand the things that perplex the young, so naturally they cannot reach them. I cannot help feeling that our churches today have turnstiles—you can go out, but there is no means of return."

He often thought, he said, "that the young brought up in homes where God is actively disapproved of are better off. They might react. It is the indifference that kills." He looked at me with a pained expression, saying, "Oh, so many pious Anglican households—empty of true religious feelings!" He thought a moment and said, "Some of the best Anglicans today are those who had been Protestants—they know what they were missing."

Upon reaching 65th Street we walked down the steps to the Zoo and began paying our respects to the seals (a good deal cooler in their pool than Eliot in his heavy winter suit), the big cats, the opossum and the hippopotamus.

We smiled at each other upon arrival at the opossum's cage. "I can see," he said, "you're thinking of *Old Possum's Book of Practical Cats!*" He looked at the creature intently, adding, "It was Ezra Pound, you know, who dubbed me 'Old Possum,' and it seemed right to use it in the title of a collection of verse so different from anything I had published before. But it has led to a lot of people inquiring as to Old Possum's identity!"

As we walked away from the hippopotamus's cage, admiring the "ugly" beast, I said that I also admired Eliot's poem "The Hippopotamus," adding that the Church *should* be attacked for its worldliness. He said, "That poem shocked many persons when it appeared—and not particularly religious persons. Today it could not possibly shock. And I suppose tomorrow it will appear in children's anthologies!" He grew quiet for a moment as we walked slowly up the steps and out of the park. "I first read 'The Hippopotamus' at a Red Cross affair. Sir Edmund Gosse was in the chair—and *he* was shocked!" After a moment, he added, "Arnold Bennett enjoyed it, and whenever we met always asked me when I was going to write another 'Hippopotamus'! It is the only poem of mine that I know Joyce read: in Paris he told me, 'I have been to the Jardin des Plantes [the Paris zoo] and paid my respects to your hippopotamus!'"

By the time we reached Fifth Avenue he had brought the matter up to date: "Since that was written I have come to serve as a church warden and know the struggle to get money in when needed. If one lives long enough, one learns!"

It was a short ride to Eliot's destination. He seemed much more relaxed than when I had picked him up a few hours before. He talked of his own parish, St. Stephen's, in Gloucester Road, in the South Kensington district of London. "You would like it," he said, and he seemed to grow very thoughtful.

"I am grateful for this interlude," he told me as the cab pulled up and we got out. "Now you must plan to come to England. Can you this year?" I replied that it did not seem likely, but that I would think about it. "Do, do. I should enjoy your company. Good-by, good-by." The second good-by wafted back to me after he had swiftly seized and shaken my hand, turned and disappeared into the dimly lit lobby.

# Chapter Four

I was ordained a deacon, the preliminary step to my becoming a priest, by the Episcopal Bishop of New York in the Cathedral of St. John the Divine on June 8, 1952.

In a letter written on July 22, Eliot referred to this, and also commented on Reinhold Niebuhr:

"I kept you in mind at Mass on Sunday the 8th of June, and ought to have written to you ere now to express my happiness in your ordination. I must thank you for your subsequent letter and also for your note of the 18th, giving me news of Reinhold Niebuhr. I am glad that he has got away to his country house. It seems to me unlikely that he will ever be able to resume activity to the full extent, but as he has been overworking himself for years, I only hope that he will have sufficient vigour and contentment for new thought and writing, even if he can no longer bear the strain of lecturing or of [here Eliot added in longhand in the margin, "such numerous"] personal contacts."

At the end of this letter, Eliot wrote, for the first time, "Yours affectionately." Thereafter, he would almost always, in one form or another, use the word "affectionately" as a closing to his letters.

In the fall of 1952, while walking with Niebuhr on Riverside Drive in New York, a weekly practice we had decided on to afford him moderate exercise during his recovery, I asked him about the foreign sale of his books, particularly imagining that he would be much read in England. He immediately registered disappointment with the treatment he had received at the hands of his English publisher. I asked him if it was possible for him to change publishers and if he had ever thought of going over to Faber & Faber. He told me that he was free to change and that he would be delighted and honored to be published by so distinguished a firm. I then asked him if he would like me to raise the matter with Eliot and he said that he would be very pleased if I would do so.

I wrote to Eliot on this matter and received the following reply on December 2, 1952:

"First, in reply to your letter of the Sunday before Advent, I am most interested in what you say about Dr. Niebuhr, and his views about the publication of his future work in this country. I will certainly discuss this suggestion of yours with my Board. Have you any idea, however, what type of work his next book is likely to be? I assume that the one called *The Irony of American History* is already committed to his present publisher. I suppose that any further work of his will take him more time than his previous books, but I certainly agree that it is a very good thing that he should have something in view now that he is no longer able to lecture and conduct seminars."

Within two weeks I received another letter from Eliot concerning Niebuhr:

"This is merely a postscript to my last letter to say that I have discussed with my colleagues, in confidence, your interesting item about Niebuhr, and I can tell you that they are keenly interested and that he would find a welcome here. As you may know, we published not long ago, his brother's *Christ and Culture* and are very pleased with ourselves for having done so."

I related this information to Niebuhr, who immediately wrote to Eliot to say that he would, indeed, like to be associated with Faber & Faber. He also sent along a copy of *The Irony of American History*. In a letter thanking him for the book, Eliot commented, "I have read it through with pleasure and with almost unqualified agreement. It seems to me a book of great sagacity and wisdom."

Niebuhr's next book and all those that followed were published by Faber & Faber.

Throughout the years of my friendship with Eliot, I enjoyed sending him gifts, particularly food, which he especially relished. That Christmas of 1952 my mother and I packed up a large gift box and mailed it off to England. Always grateful and considerate of other people's feelings, he wrote my mother the following letter on December 27. It was the first of many letters she was to receive.

"I was very much touched by all your bounty: first the parcel with a Cake and a magnificent Cheese, and then the box containing the gay Candle—far too fine to burn for a long time to come: I can't bear the idea of letting that jewelled Christmas tree burn away!—and the Fudge. I believe the one appropriate adjective for such Fudge, if my memories of childhood are correct, is *scrumptious*. It is being demolished and done away with, but *slowly,* and appreciatively.

"You and William are very good to me, and it is very little that I have ever done for him except feel a warm affection towards him. I like to get his letters, and hear of his activities and his joy in them.

"I look forward in hope that I may have a less fleeting glimpse of you and Mr. Levy when I am next in New York. I expect to be over for a few weeks in June, but I doubt whether New York will see anything of me on this trip, as I have to go straight to St. Louis, and on my way back try to get a couple of weeks with my sisters in Boston and be in London again by the beginning of July. But I shall not fail to let William know of my movements, and I hope we may have a meeting. Meanwhile, all blessings on your household for the coming year."

I was to have the opportunity of seeing Eliot at that time; indeed, during his brief stay in New York, I was the only person he saw.

After his visit to St. Louis, and after I had been ordained a priest, Eliot wrote to me on June 20, 1953, from Cambridge, Massachusetts, where he was staying with his sister-in-law, Theresa G. Eliot (Mrs. Henry Ware Eliot):

"Thank you for your letter, which had to be forwarded to me here, as I had left St. Louis to spend a couple of nights in Washington. I am here until the 26th, when to Connecticut for two nights with cousins; and I shall be in New York on Sunday night the 28th. As I leave after lunch on Monday, by air to London, you will see that there is not much time. But you might telephone me on Sunday night or about 8 to 9 on

Monday morning the 29th, and we will see whether it is possible to squeeze in a moment somewhere. In my brief stay in Cambridge my timetable has been wholly filled by visits to relatives and a few old friends."

Eliot added, "You are now a Priest. May God give you all strength for the most arduous of all vocations."

In New York, Eliot stayed with his publisher and friend Robert Giroux. I called him there, precisely at eight on the morning of the twenty-ninth.

"Mr. Eliot, this is William."

"Ah, William! I have been expecting your call."

"I know your time is limited today...."

"I have saved the morning altogether. Could you meet me at ten-thirty at my publisher's office, Harcourt, Brace and Company, on Madison Avenue?"

I told him that I could.

Mr. Eliot arrived five minutes late. I knew him well enough by this time not to be surprised when on that hot, sunny July day in New York, I saw him hurry toward me carrying an umbrella and wearing a heavy woolen suit.

"William!"

As I rose from the deep leather armchair of the outer office, Eliot took off a hat that I recognized at once as a "wopsical hat," a term he had coined in one of his poems.

"I've arranged for us to have a quiet place to talk," he told me while shaking my hand.

A young man introduced himself to Eliot as one of the editors and then quickly and with an air of efficiency led us to a luxurious air-conditioned office, obviously belonging to the top echelon executive of the publishing house.

[35]

"Is there anything more I can do for you, Mr. Eliot?" the editor asked.

"No, thank you. You've been most helpful," was Eliot's response.

The young editor smiled pleasantly, if a bit sheepishly, was noticeably flattered and fumbled with the doorknob as he closed the door.

I had witnessed once more a reaction I would often see, namely, that people treated Eliot with extreme deference. He accepted this without relishing it, as though it were a necessary and not too unpleasant burden. However, a certain weariness in his manner revealed his feeling that such decorum and self-consciousness delayed the business at hand.

People who went out of their way to assist Eliot usually got in his way. After one such occasion he said to me with an incredulous smile, "I have long observed that poets are expected to be helpless as infants," and added with a chuckle, "in this case a rather—uh—large infant!"

Slowly and with great care, Eliot surveyed the room, his eyes finally resting on a green leather sofa. Gesturing to it, he cocked his head in my direction, smiled broadly, and, with the third finger of his left hand, pushed up the horn-rimmed glasses that had slipped down onto his nose.

It was the first time I had seen Eliot in glasses, and they were, like the man himself, distinctive—the temple pieces growing out of the center of the circular frame, not the top, as is usual. I later observed that he would wear them in an unpredictable fashion, sometimes for reading, sometimes at dinner, sometimes on the street, but he would unfailingly handle them awkwardly as if using them for the very first time. In fact, he handled all objects in a clumsy way—even, oddly enough, his own fountain pen and pocket watch. His slow and careful use of objects was not methodical, as I originally had thought, but, instead, painstaking. All physical chores, even the putting on and taking off of an overcoat, seemed to Eliot to offer a resistance which he had to combat. It was for this reason, in part, that I thought of him as a man not associated with objects or possessions. His mind was his sole possession, and I always thought of him as cerebral rather than physical. His body was almost an encumbrance.

Now, with his eyeglasses temporarily back in place (they would slip down periodically during our conversation, only to be pushed back involuntarily), Eliot asked, "Would this sofa be comfortable for you?" I replied that it would suit me fine and asked where he planned to sit. He pondered the question for a moment, then advanced to a large leather armchair and proceeded, laboriously, to draw it up to the sofa. I helped him, and soon we were both comfortably settled in our respective places. A moment later, however, Eliot rose, removed his suit jacket and began to place it over the back of a chair. I asked, "Do you think it safe? I mean . . . you're warm now and the air conditioning is so cool in here. You might catch cold."

Eliot raised his eyebrows, nodded his head once and agreed, "You're right!" put on his jacket and resumed his seat.

I was wearing my clerical collar. Eliot pointed to it, adding emphasis as he said, "How good to see you thus!" He smiled warmly and continued, "I am sorry I couldn't be at your ordination, but I held you in my prayers."

I reminded him that it was his writing and example that had

[37]

first directed my thoughts toward the Church and that he was partly responsible for the decision I had made.

"Yes," he acknowledged willingly, and then added with a chuckle, "and I shall have to keep an eye on your career—especially if you should go liberal on me, or something like that!"

I laughed.

Eliot continued, "Will you take a parish now?"

"No, I prefer to continue teaching college," was my reply.

"I am sure that you could easily have a parish if you wanted one and that you would make a worthy contribution there, but I cannot help being glad that you want to teach. Teaching is an honorable profession and we have too few good teachers today. I am continually appalled by the declining level of education."

Eliot used the arms of his chair to support the bulk of his weight as he adjusted himself more comfortably in the chair. "Will you teach the Bible in your English courses?"

"Yes," I replied, "it's in the curriculum."

"Good. Your theological training will help you there."

Eliot's expression suddenly changed. He now frowned, creating a deep cleft between his eyebrows, and told me, "I recently spoke at a university in their so-called Chapel that was built for all denominations and, as a result, expresses none. Such buildings ought not to be constructed because they do not serve any religion. They merely create an impression of a religious atmosphere that is *ersatz*." Eliot accentuated the word, raising his eyebrows at the same time.

In my friendship with Eliot I learned that he would rather have seen a total absence of religion in the world than a semblance of it that served only a social purpose.

Returning to the subject of teaching, I told Eliot that I had my students read Graham Greene's *The Power and the Glory* because they could understand religious ideas and attitudes more easily when they discovered them growing out of the novel's action. Eliot agreed that it was a fine book and a good example of the kind of material worth teaching and discussing. We talked particularly about the scene in the one-room jailhouse where Greene brilliantly shows up prudery as pride.

"I have not yet read his latest book, *The End of the Affair,* but I have heard so much about it I feel as though I had. Yes, I liked *The Power and the Glory,* but *The Heart of the Matter* . . . he imposed his, uh, unpleasant material, and I question his orthodoxy—but correctness is a better word—in dealing with the issues."

Next, I told Eliot that I owed him a debt of gratitude for introducing me to the work of Simone Weil. He was pleased that I shared his admiration for her ideas, and added, "Another great mind is, as you probably know, that of Martin Buber. I felt his undeniable greatness the first time I met him, a thing I do not often feel."

I agreed with Eliot that *I and Thou* was the most significant book for Christians by this Jewish theologian, and that it had had a profound effect on modern religious thought. I told Eliot of my attending a lecture by Buber and being so enthralled by his thinking aloud that I completely forgot to take notes! We then agreed, humorously, that this short, heavy-set, bald, bearded genius resembled the Nome King in one of the Oz books.

I was interested in learning of Eliot's present work and asked, "When will *The Confidential Clerk* open in London?"

"Some time in September, I understand. It will have its first performance at the Edinburgh Festival on August twenty-fifth," he replied. "We have no New York plans yet."

"Will you attend the rehearsals?"

"Yes, yes, I always do."

Once again, Eliot shifted his position in the deep armchair and then cupped his chin in his hand. "I think it is my best play—so far," he added, the latter with a twinkle in his eye. "At least at this moment it is good. Later will come the doubts. *The Confidential Clerk* is less complicated on the surface than *The Cocktail Party,* but has much more in layers to be meditated on and thought of as meanings of life. It will probably seem less profound to many, but it is really much more so."

Eliot leaned against the back of the chair, relaxed, and said, less seriously, "In any case, I will be anxious to know what you make of it. You know, in *The Cocktail Party,* I mention the saffron monkey. I was just having fun! But, one critic in the *Hudson Review* found out about a monkey-worshiping tribe and wrote an entire thesis based on that!" Eliot threw his head back and laughed. "I never had the slightest idea such a thing existed!"

Reflecting on rehearsals, Eliot said, "I come to them prepared to question lines—rewrite some and cut others. The actors are very helpful. They say to the director, 'This line is impossible to say,' or 'I don't know what this means,' and practically all of the time they are right, and I rewrite the lines to suit them. Playwriting is not something you can complete in a study; it is a communal enterprise. After all, a play belongs to the performing arts. It is not something to be read; it is

[*40*]

meant to be seen on the stage. One has to accept this responsibility if one writes a play. It *is* a communal enterprise. And I like working with the actors, too. I thought Alec Guinness in *The Cocktail Party* was superb, perfect, the ideal realization of the part I had written. And you know," he said smiling happily, "the irrepressible Irish humor that he added brought immeasurable interest to the part and to the play. I was delighted! But, in contrast, the actor who replaced him played it much too heavy-handedly. Irene Worth was excellent. John Gielgud," he reminisced, "wanted to play Harry Monchensey in *The Family Reunion,* but I was opposed to it on the grounds that he wasn't religious enough to finally understand the motivation of the character. But, we were talking about *The Confidential Clerk.* It will come as a surprise to the audience. It is much simpler than anything I have done and, you might say, a departure."

I mentioned the *Four Quartets.*

"I stand or fall on them," Eliot stated emphatically.

I asked him the meaning of one of the lines in "Little Gidding" and showed it to him. He read the following silently and thoughtfully:

> *You are here to kneel*
> *Where prayer has been valid.*

Then he looked up and said, "What I mean is that for some of us, a sense of place is compelling. If it is a religious place, a place made special by the sacrifice of a martyrdom, then it retains an aura. We know that once before a man gave of himself *here* and was accepted *here,* and it was so important that the occasion continues to invest the place with its holiness. Of course, William, I am aware that not all persons have a sense of place (as I describe it), nor is it necessary for it to exist to make prayer valid."

I was moved to say that I knew what he felt. That to me, to kneel at an altar which had been in continuous use in an English cathedral for, say, eight hundred years, infused a quality of awe and a sense of historic continuity into the Mass.

"Exactly," Eliot replied.

I asked, "And that was part of your early response to England, then?"

"It was," he replied, and seemed lost for a moment in meditation. I was satisfied with what I had learned and did not pursue the subject.

A knock at the door, and Eliot was reminded that he had a few things to attend to before lunch and departure for the airport.

He turned to me, took up the first editions of the *Four Quartets* by my side (each of the four poems printed separately) and carried them to a desk. Sitting down, he began the slow, laborious task of inscribing, signing and dating each one. His patience was endless. I said I liked to have a dated memento of each of our meetings. "You shall have them then," he affirmed.

Eliot finished writing in the first poem and then reached for the second. "I should protest," I began; "I only meant for you to sign one, but I wanted to show you my entire set."

Eliot looked up, his glasses perched on the end of his nose once again and said, "It would do you no good!"

A moment later he interrupted his signing to say, "On my next trip I will be in New York longer. Then I will hope to see something of your mother and father. I liked meeting them and would like to know them better. But this time, this way of a night in New York at each end of the trip seemed best. If you see a few people, you please them less than you displease those you do not see. It is better to see no one."

I smiled at being defined as "no one," and said how sensitive I was to his kindness in seeing me. He countered, "I wanted to."

When he had signed the Quartet *The Dry Salvages* after correcting a misprint (*horseshoe* for *hermit* crab! in the nineteenth line of the first part) and initialing it, he rose and walked me to the office door. I stopped to tell Eliot how much I enjoyed being with him. He replied, "It is nice to be liked not only for your poems."

I said I'd plan to come to England in a year or two.

"Good. I will take you with me to an abbey I stay at on occasion. The abbot is a friend of mine. One day I will go there to stay, permanently. It suits me. I would have no guests then, but you could come every year for a week or two, being a priest."

We shook hands warmly, and as his last words sank into my mind I was deeply moved by the permanence of the bond between us. Then I opened the door and walked swiftly away, aware that several persons rushed into the office where Eliot was.

## Chapter Five

"I've received another letter from Mr. Eliot," my mother told me excitedly as she entered my room carrying the morning mail. It was dated October 5, 1953, and read as follows:

"I want to thank you, first for your birthday card (I don't know how you knew when my birthday was, to time it so well!) and second, for a wonderful box of good things to eat, which I take to be a birthday present also. Such gifts are more appreciated as one gets older, and certainly on one's 65th birthday. [Eliot was born in St. Louis, Missouri, on September 26, 1888.] I do not know why you should be so kind to me.

"I owe many letters to William, in response to letters and enclosures from him. But my life is still a very crowded one: at 65 one begins to find that everything takes more time, including answering letters; and one has not yet reached the age, or the stage of obvious infirmity, at which people expect less of one. (That is why I am proposing to take a long holiday, of a sea voyage, of two months January and February). I should however like William to know, that even if I do not answer all of his letters, I should be sorry if he wrote less frequently, since I like to feel in touch with him and his progress in his vocation.

"The next time I come to New York, I expect to spend a few days there and hope to see you and Mr. Levy again. Indeed, I do not consider that I visited New York at all, this year: it was merely a momentary halt between visits to St. Louis and Boston, and I saw no one there except my host of one night and William himself."

In September I had finished writing *William Barnes: The Man and the Poems* and had received my doctor's degree from Columbia University. At that time I sent the typescript to Eliot because he had invited me to do so and because I was eager to have him read it and offer a judgment.

It came as a surprise and a compliment to me that he had submitted it to Faber & Faber for consideration.

I also sent him the latest Walt Kelly book. I had the pleasure of introducing Eliot to Pogo and through the years sent him each new volume as it appeared. In the following letter, dated December 14, 1953, he commented on both books.

"I am writing at last about your book on William Barnes. I read it myself with both enjoyment and profit, coming to it as a reader with no previous acquaintance with Barnes's work. I must say I found the book interesting and well written, and the quotations, which are plentiful, extremely helpful—indeed, they gave me a much higher impression of Barnes as a poet than I had expected to receive. His poetry is also interesting because it seems to me that he must have had a considerable influence on Thomas Hardy. I am not a particular admirer of Hardy myself, and I therefore find I like some of Barnes's poems, as you quote them, more than anything I have read of Hardy's. This does not mean, of course, that I regard him as a better poet than Hardy—I don't think he is—but simply that I find him more congenial, and I was impressed also by the technical achievement of some of his verse forms.

"Now the book has been read by two other readers here, but while their opinion of it was favourable, the Board felt that there was not likely to be enough demand for your book to justify their adding it to what is always about as heavy a load as we can carry. I wonder whether you have offered it to any New York publisher yet? If you could find a publisher at home, I should think that some publisher in this country might be prepared to take sheets, because the book seems to me a very informative introduction to Barnes's work. I think that you have much more chance of finding an English publisher, if you find one in New York first.

"I am holding the typescript until we hear from you, as you might wish to name some other publisher to whom we could send it. Alternatively, you might like a literary agent to attempt to place it on your behalf.

"To turn to a lighter matter, I very much enjoyed the 'Pogo Papers' which you inscribed for me. Apart from the interesting glimpses of wild life in the Bayou country, I was much interested in the type of drawing, the type of humour, and the idiom of the text. I should say that Mr. Kelly must have been influenced, directly or indirectly, by James Joyce's *Finnegans*

[46]

*Wake.* The type of wordplay and punning, although skillfully adapted to a more popular audience than Joyce has ever enjoyed, seemed to me of the same order. Perhaps it is partly that Mr. Kelly, who is presumably an Irishman, has something of the same temperament and feeling for words as Joyce. The drawings seem to me to show a lineal descent from the work of two early American masters of caricature, both well before your time, that is Goldberg and George Herriman. It is just possible that you may be acquainted with Krazy Kat. Kelly has, in fact, much more affinity with these draughtsmen than with Walt Disney. To judge from the 'Pogo Papers', I find Kelly more sympathetic than Disney, in much of whose work I detect what seems to me a streak of cruelty.

"There is also in the general area of the grotesque a remote kinship with the peculiar nonsense verses of the German poet, Christian Morgenstern. I do not suppose, however, that Mr. Kelly has ever heard of Morgenstern. The point here, however, is that there is something about both the drawing and humour which is more Central European than Anglo-Saxon. I am dimly aware that there is a good deal of topical allusion, some of a political nature, which escapes me, though J did not fail to perceive that one of the characters is closely related to Senator McCarthy.

"I am sending you a kind of Christmas card which is a copy of a lecture [*The Three Voices of Poetry*] I recently delivered. It has been printed as a pamphlet and won't arrive, I suppose, until after Christmas, so this letter carries with it my most affectionate regards, the reminder of my constant thoughts, and my most cordial greetings to your father and mother."

[47]

In March, 1954, I was elated to receive a presentation copy of *The Confidential Clerk* mailed from London. A year or two later, Eliot would take some pains explaining to me about books signed by him: "If someone who has a claim on my time or attention offers me a book to be autographed, I do so with just my name. In a second category are books in which I write 'inscribed to'—that means I know the person and he or she has brought me a copy of the book to be inscribed. Usually I put in no more than their name. In the third category are presentation copies—books I give to an individual that are signed 'to' or 'for' the person—of these there is a very limited number."

Shortly after receiving the book, I heard in a news report on the radio that Eliot had suffered a serious heart attack and was in the London Clinic. I sent a telegram, flowers and a series of notes. In the following letter of May 11, I was reassured:

"I have now returned from the London Clinic to my flat, and if my doctor is satisfied when I see him tomorrow, I am to go off for a fortnight's seaside convalescence on Saturday. I am afraid that my friends in America got a very misleading report of my state of health from the radio—an announcement which apparently was due to a wholly unjustified statement in an evening newspaper here. There is nothing organically wrong with my heart, and the tachycardia was something purely nervous, and in that way rather obscure in origin. I am now obliged to take things rather easily until the autumn. That is all."

During the summer I was priest-in-charge of All Angels' Church in New York City. Eliot commented on this, on the death of one of my dear friends, and discussed, in the following letter, dated August 21, 1954, theology and churchmanship:

"I was pleased by your writing to me on the Feast of the Transfiguration: a very special feast to my mind and one that I prefer to regard as a Day of Obligation (as I believe it is in the Eastern Orthodox Churches). Your news was very welcome: excellent that you should have been priest-in-charge for the last two months, and that you should presently be having your holiday (though a very brief one) in Arlington [Vermont] with your family.

"I was very sorry to learn of the death of your friend [Bridget Ryan of Devon, England]. You are quite right in saying that our ties are not formed quantitatively, by the amount of time spent in our friends' company; and that 'meeting' of the right quality can affect a lifetime. What does count, however, is Time: when one has a true friendship, it is a happiness to think of the years that it has endured. But friendship is largely shared experience, and experience can be shared on various levels of consciousness.

"It seems to me a very good thing to start in Low Churchmanship and to find oneself moving towards higher churchmanship. For the movement should come from the inside, I think: so that, as one's devotion and one's theological understanding grow, the outer forms will come to appear as the right form of expression. That is the contrary of the 'aesthetic' high churchmanship which cares more for the forms than for the spiritual and intellectual content. The Tractarians themselves were by no means very High Churchmen in ritual. But it is good to see how the Veneration of the B.V.M. [Blessed Virgin Mary], for instance, *fits in* inevitably to Catholic doc-

[49]

trine: to see it as naturally growing out of the Faith, instead of something added on to it.

"Did I mention that when I went to South Africa I took with me Tillich's Systematic Theology Vol. 1, and that it seems to me one of the profoundest theological works of recent times? It is good to be able to learn from a Lutheran. But after two readings I can still not say where I *agree* and *disagree:* even if I disagreed with all of it, eventually, it would still be a book which had helped me to understand the problems with which it deals.

"I had a note from Niebuhr. His book is very good, indeed, and I am happy to have been able to publish it here: but I look forward very eagerly to the greater work on which he is engaged.

"And now the POGO books have come: and will give me a feast of irresponsible and gay language for some time to come. Thank you warmly."

A few weeks later I received another letter, this one written on Whitsunday (the Feast of the Holy Ghost), in which Eliot thanked me for blessing and sending him a small angel's head segment of a stained-glass window that had been removed from All Angels' Church. In this letter I perceived Eliot's preoccupation with health. Although not a true hypochondriac, Eliot was unnaturally concerned over the state of his health. This manifested itself in the taking of a considerable number of pills which he carried loose in his lower left vest pocket. At my home I observed him, while having a drink before dinner, popping a number of them into his mouth. I never questioned him about this, but he volunteered, "This will help my digestion." Eliot was not addicted to pills, however, and I am certain that he never used any form of narcotic.

Eliot did suffer from bronchitis, and found he needed, as stated in this letter, to be out of England's damp and chilly climate in the winter:

"This is merely a Whitsun greeting, with my prayer for you this day—my first Communion since Mid-Lent, for the priest who came to the Clinic on Easter Day had to come rather late, and my breakfast and medicine could not be retarded that long. You have probably been celebrating, yourself, this morning.

"The piece of glass arrived quite safely, and is lying on my mantelpiece. Thank you for it. It will be valued.

"I have made good progress, with two weeks convalescence at the seaside before Whitsun. It was strange, and hard to bear, to have to lie in bed during Holy Week and over Easter, but even this sort of deprivation, I think, can be regarded as a penance: and the whole illness—though apparently of nervous origin, and involving no organic lesion whatever—so that my life will not be shortened by a day—comes as a reminder that after one has passed middle age one must be, in one sense, a little 'retired' from life: that there may remain just as important things to do (please God)—but that one must not try to do so many things, or *waste* any of the time that is left—and that one must husband one's strength for the things that matter most. When one is young it is right to dissipate and even squander one's resources of strength and time to some extent —for one should not be too sure that one knows in what directions one can be most useful. Many activities that I once pursued, which 'sensible' people would have said at the time were a waste of time for *me,* proved useful in my own education and development. But when a man is over 60, he should have learned by experience what to say Yes or No to, and to say No much more often than Yes. The things I can do well, I *believe* I can do as well as ever—only, it takes more time, to do them well; and therefore I can't afford to be so active in other ways.

"I shan't be in New York before next spring. I shall have my sister with me through July, and that will be a great happiness, if her health is good; in September I may visit some of my oldest friends who live in Geneva; and later I must go to Hamburg to take a Prize. Probably, I shall spend part of January and February in some better climate (though not so far away or so expensive a journey as South Africa, nor do I wish to go to a country with such unhappy race problems) and I hope to come over to America in the Spring.

"I am glad that Reinhold Niebuhr can be so active. I have been reading his contributions to the *New Leader,* which I see regularly. Give him my warm regards. I hope Niebuhr is pleased by the appearance of his book—I mean, by the way we produced it.

"I send herewith my affectionate Whitsun greetings to your parents. Although I have only met them on that one occasion, I have come to think of them as old friends."

Months passed and I received occasional letters from Eliot. I learned that he was in fine health except for an attack of arthritis in one shoulder which he dealt with through massage, although he complained it "takes more time—going to and fro to the masseur—than I can really afford."

He later reported, "My health continues good, though I find it always more of a struggle to keep up with day to day obligations and to get any constructive work done." During this time he did finish his Goethe address for Hamburg and also a poem, "The Cultivation of Christmas Trees," a copy of which he sent me for Christmas 1954, commenting, "I do not consider it very well executed, but I hope that the idea is a right one."

That fall, E. McKnight Kauffer, the artist and illustrator, in whose apartment Eliot and I had had our second meeting, died. After reading the obituary in *The New York Times,* I went to the funeral parlor on Madison Avenue and signed the condolence book: "T. S. Eliot, signed for him by" and my own name. I wrote to tell Eliot of this and of my prayers at the altar the following Sunday. He replied:

"This is no more than an acknowledgement of your letter of October 25, and to thank you for remembering Ted Kauffer. He was a sad and very lovable soul, who had lost attachment to this life, without I fear any very positive hope of another, and he needs praying for. I shall miss him very much, though on my last two visits to New York I had not seen him, and he was a very poor correspondent."

Eliot's health continued to improve. His doctor advised him to stop smoking, however, which he reluctantly did, eating candy as a substitute. It was a new luxury for him. He told me once that his puritanical upbringing had left him permanently scarred with an inability to indulge this pleasure. Indeed, when he was a boy, he told me, although he had the money he could never bring himself to enter a candy store and actually purchase a box of candy for himself. Now, some sixty years later, he wrote my mother on December 27, 1954, acknowledging a large box of candy which she had sent:

"Thank you very much for the beautiful box of candy which reached me at the right time and was opened on Christmas Day. Formerly, I wasn't much of a sweet-eater, and gave most of what I was given away; but now that I have given up smoking, I eat more of everything, including candy when I get it (I was brought up to believe that it was selfish indulgence to buy candy for *oneself*!) with the result that I am getting much fatter—which pleases my doctor, and also my tailor."

For Christmas that year I sent Eliot an octagonal blue tile about three and a half inches across, bearing in relief a white profile portrait of Abraham Lincoln. It had been given me by my favorite uncle when I was six years old. I had used it as a paperweight. I knew Eliot would delight in something American, and I wanted to give him something I truly valued. He acknowledged it in the following way:

"I was very much touched by your Christmas present (which was so well packed, and arrived quite undamaged) and by what you told me about it. With all the associations that it has for you, it becomes a very important and significant gift: so important that one shrinks from accepting it, except that to refuse to accept would be to undervalue the intention of the giver, and betray an unkind misunderstanding. It is a charming tile in itself; and it takes my mind back to the steel engraving of a portrait of Lincoln, which hung in our front hall when I was a child. My grandfather had known him slightly (for he was very active on the Northern side, in Missouri during the Civil War, and was a member of the Western Sanitary Commission, which looked after the medical services of the Army and Fleet on the Mississippi) and we were brought up to reverence his memory."

Eliot wrote me that he would be in New York again in May. I had decided that I wanted to receive a crucifix from

Eliot. So I asked him for one, assuming, of course, that he might have an extra crucifix or could obtain one easily. I had underestimated him. I hadn't realized that Eliot would take this matter so seriously. He wrote on Easter Monday, 1955:

"There is, it seems, only one shop in London which might have a crucifix which I would be satisfied to give you. If I can get there before I leave, I will see what they have. And if I like nothing there, I should prefer to wait—as you have held out hopes of being in England again, for a visit, which I pray may be realised—as I have been told that there is a former pupil of Eric Gill who could make a good crucifix for me. I have three crucifixes, but all given me by friends, so that I cannot give any of them away while I live.

"I am not sure what size crucifix you want: size for the wall, over a bed or a prayer desk, or smaller or larger.

"I shall be in New York from the 11th to the 16th May only, but I hope for a glimpse of you then. And I want very much, if I can, to get out to see the Niebuhrs. For your private information, I shall be staying again with Robert Giroux."

Our next meeting would be a memorable one. Not only would he meet my parents once again and spend an entire Sunday afternoon, including dinner, at our home, but he would bring with him the most handsome crucifix I had ever seen, a gift symbolizing the sharing of a common Faith.

## Chapter Six

The telephone rang three times before it was answered.

"Hello?"

"Hello. This is William Turner Levy. May I please speak to Mr. Eliot?"

"Father Levy, this is Robert Giroux. Mr. Eliot is expecting your call."

After a short wait, Eliot said, "Here I am, William. How promptly you have called. I look forward to seeing you and your family on Sunday. At what time will you pick me up?"

I replied, "I thought you might like to go to St. Mary the Virgin's at eleven, so I should pick you up at ten-thirty."

"I will be ready. Let me write this down—ten-thirty."

I said, "Or do you have another choice?"

"No, that will be perfect, William."

True to Eliot's customary brevity on the telephone, all was arranged with an economy of time and words. Before he could hang up, I interposed, "I'm seeing you tonight—at the Y.M.H.A. I've never heard you do a reading."

Eliot answered, "I am hopeful to rise and do the right thing. It will be all poetry, you know. Do you want to hear any poem in particular?"

I was unprepared for the question, but quickly replied, "I'd like to hear the one you sent me for Christmas, 'The Cultivation of Christmas Trees.' "

"Well . . . yes, I could do that . . . any other?"

"I'd like to hear a reading of an early poem, preferably 'Portrait of a Lady,' if that is possible."

" 'Portrait of a Lady.' My, your requests are unusual, William. But I will think about it. Good! And then I will see you on Sunday."

I thanked him, wished him a pleasant stay, and offered to give him my telephone number again, which he refused, saying it was in his book.

That evening, Eliot began the program with a magnificent reading of "Portrait of a Lady," prefaced with the remark, "I might have read this well forty years ago, but no one asked me to read it then." The last poem he read that evening was "The Cultivation of Christmas Trees," which he announced he was reading in public for the first time.

On Sunday morning I kept the cab waiting in front of Robert Giroux's apartment house, knowing that Eliot would be ready to leave immediately.

Mr. Giroux answered the door. "Father Levy? I'm Robert Giroux. This is the first time we've met," he said cordially as he extended his hand. We shook hands and then Mr. Giroux stepped to one side, saying, "Come in."

I heard Eliot's ringing voice, "Here I am, William!" Eliot was standing in the center of the living room. "I am ready to go." I was amused: Eliot was obviously ready. He was wearing a heavy overcoat and a dark red scarf, and holding a hat in his left hand.

He strode to meet me, grasped my hand tightly, and said, "Now, I have something I must put into your hands." He led me to a leather satchel in the bedroom. He zipped open the top and produced from it a paper bag which he handed to me, saying, "Here is your crucifix. I am sorry it is not properly wrapped, but I had to show it to customs."

I removed the crucifix from the bag. The figure was of silver and mounted on walnut. I looked up to thank Eliot and saw that he was beaming. Neither of us spoke for a long moment, and then he squared his shoulders and announced, "We must be off!"

At the door Eliot told Mr. Giroux, "Do not worry, I shall be in very good hands today."

Settled in the cab, I once again took out the crucifix, and told Eliot how much I liked it, adding, "You were able to get one to your liking, after all."

Eliot smiled and replied, "Yes, when I first considered finding one for you, I consulted Sir Herbert Read, who advised that only Dunstan Pruden, one of Eric Gill's students, was producing anything suitable. He recommended a religious art shop which might have one, and told me that if I could not find one there, he would undertake to get one from Pruden directly. I was not able to get to the gallery until the day before I sailed, but found exactly what I had hoped for. I am glad you like it. I must add that in the rush I had no time to have it blessed. But that is something you can do yourself."

It was a warm day. Aware of Eliot's heavy coat, I asked him if he would like me to open a window. To my surprise, he replied, "No, thank you, William. I am perfectly comfortable."

In the Church of St. Mary the Virgin, Eliot took out his small leather-bound prayer book and read from the psalms and other prayers of preparation. He then studied the leaflet, and I handed him a hymnal open to the first hymn, which both of us knew and loved, John Keble's "Lord, in thy name thy servants plead." We smiled at each other in recognition when we saw that selection, as we did once again when we were about to sing Cardinal Newman's "Praise to the Holiest in the Height." Eliot sang well in a low voice, and made the responses audibly but modestly. He occasionally supported his large frame when standing by placing his hands on the top of the pew in front. He listened to the sermon by sitting all the way back in the pew and hunching forward, his big hands spread on his knees, his eyes studying his shoes.

On the way out, I introduced Eliot to the rector, the Reverend Dr. Grieg Taber: "Father Taber, I'd like to present Mr. T. S. Eliot, senior warden of St. Stephen's Church, South Kensington."

"I recognize you, Mr. Eliot," Father Taber said. "It is a great honor to have you with us."

Eliot smiled and said, "This was a beautiful service, Father Taber."

As I hailed a cab, two young ladies leaving the church approached me and said, "That's T. S. Eliot, isn't it? We heard him read on Friday night at the Y.M.H.A."

I said, "Yes," and asked if they would like to be introduced. They gave me their names—both were students at Barnard College—and I introduced them to Eliot. He was pleased, saying to me, once we got settled in the cab, "It is nice to meet people who are interested in your work. They apparently enjoyed the reading."

Eliot told me that he always enjoyed reading his poetry at the Young Men's Hebrew Association in New York, where he had read two nights before. "It is a very good, responsive audience," he told me. "It is made up mostly of students and young people who know the poems and I can sense their response. It is very gratifying. Although they pay me only a fraction of what I am paid elsewhere, I will always read for them because I like the audiences, and because they had me read long before today's more lucrative offers materialized."

I asked him if readings were sometimes disappointing—because of the audience. "Oh yes, particularly when there is applause before the poem is concluded—just because you pause for effect! This can be true of a fashionable audience that is comprised of persons almost totally ignorant of your work. Of course, one tries to avoid such occasions, but it is not always possible to know in advance."

We made one stop on the way to my home. I explained to Eliot that I had to conduct a baptism at All Angels' Church at twelve-thirty, an arrangement I had set up before knowing of his impending visit. Eliot was delighted to accompany me and even suggested that he be a witness. The family was overwhelmed. After the service, Eliot signed the infant's baptismal forms. Today the girl is thirteen years old and has just read *Murder in the Cathedral* at school.

In another cab, we proceeded north on the Henry Hudson

Parkway. Eliot frequently looked at the river, but said nothing.

Somehow we found ourselves talking of heaven. There had been a reference to it in the sermon. "It is possible to think of it in the most cloying, unattractive terms," Eliot said. "The prospect held out to us is almost like that of a fly shut up in a jam jar."

I added that it was a most difficult teaching task—in the pulpit—to wean people away from childish or unworthy conceptions of the demands of the Faith.

"We invent personal dogmas," Eliot reflected, "like the puritanical ideas rampant in my youth. We place prohibitions on the use of tobacco or alcohol or forbid dancing or reading certain books, and in obeying these rules we think we are accomplishing something morally worth while. It is all nonsense, of course: the substituting of easy commandments for the real ones. Our Lord said that many shall cast out devils in his name, only to be told at the last day that they are rejected by God—naturally, for the devils they cast out were not real, but of their own invention."

As the Parkway rose in elevation and we crossed the Henry Hudson Bridge, spanning Spuyten Duyvil, the point where the Harlem River flows into the Hudson and Manhattan Island ends, Eliot commented on the height and beauty of the location. Soon we were at the apartment house.

In the lobby, I could see at once, by the expression on Eliot's face, that he distrusted self-service elevators. I made light of our having to go to the eleventh floor by saying, "I enjoy being on the top floor—for the air and the view and the privacy—and because it's as close to heaven as I'm likely to get!"

Eliot's face grew serious. He thought for a moment and then said, very quietly, "You are in for a very pleasant surprise," adding, "Yes, indeed!"

My parents greeted Eliot with a warmth he reciprocated. They were about his age, and the three of them shared many attitudes.

The apartment looked very inviting in the brilliant early afternoon light. The red rug and drapes in the living room were warm against a fern-green wall, the silver glinted, thousands of book bindings added color, and Mother had placed Easter lilies, yellow chrysanthemums and lilacs in strategic places.

Judy, the family cat, advanced to greet an admirer; Eliot stooped, mumbled soft sounds, and won a cat's approval.

As he entered my study, which we used for serving cocktails informally, he exclaimed, "This is your room, just as I imagined it would be—all pictures and books!"

I took his coat, invited him to freshen up, and went to break out the ice. Returning a few minutes later, I found Eliot gazing out of my window at the river. He turned and said to me with a grin, "Sweet Thames, run softly."

I recognized Spenser's words, which Eliot had used in *The Waste Land,* and smiled.

Eliot turned to the window again and remarked, "How fortunate it is that you live on a great river. I live in Chelsea, on the Thames, as you know, and when I was a boy I was close to the Mississippi."

"The Hudson is even more beautiful up north, at Hyde Park. Franklin Roosevelt always said that he found solace in its quiet and unchanging flow," I said.

Eliot nodded and replied, "I can understand that."

My parents entered the room and, along with Eliot, took comfortable seats. Eliot sat on the small sofa next to my mother, while my father sat across from them. A low table was in between.

I showed my mother and father the crucifix Eliot had given me and together the four of us decided upon the right place in the room to hang it.

I asked Eliot what he would like to drink.

He replied uncertainly, "I would prefer just to have fruit juice, William."

I was surprised and asked, "Don't you drink at all? We have almost anything you might like, and we planned on champagne with dinner."

"Well, in that case," he said, "I would like to have a glass of champagne now, if I may." He turned to my parents and explained, "My doctor has recommended that I drink spirits cautiously, so I only have champagne on occasion. It seems to do me the least injury."

I brought martinis for my father, mother and myself, and a chilled bottle of English Market champagne—Charles Heidsieck 1949—for Eliot, who told me, much to my delight and surprise, that it was his favorite brand. We toasted Eliot as our guest; then he stood up and returned the compliment.

Conversation was easy and natural. Noticing a standing lamp next to him that was a replica of an oil lamp, Eliot commented that it was identical in design to one he had had in his room at college. Eliot was always particularly aware of details and displayed a remarkable memory of them.

Discussing his recent travels, Eliot said, "Although my body is here, I feel that my mind is two days behind. It is one of the penalties of traveling. It is not easy to travel out of England, you know. The government does not allow me to take any money out of the country. In order to be able to visit my family and a few friends here, I have to earn my way by lecturing or giving readings." (After 1957 these restrictions varied.)

I asked, "Which do you prefer to do, lecture or read?"

Without hesitation, he responded, "Lecture. There is the work beforehand writing the lecture—and I write it in three drafts—but then the delivery is easy. Normally, I can use the same lecture twice, once in England and once here. The poetry readings take more out of me and frequently leave me physically exhausted. Getting back to the money aspect, however, I recall that a number of years ago when I had less money than I have now, if I was in New York and wanted to go down to St. Elizabeth's Hospital in Washington to see Ezra Pound, I had to manage somehow to get a date to read in order to foot the bill!"

At Eliot's request, I took down several pictures from the wall and showed them to him. He especially liked the English watercolors by Ruskin, Cox, Sandby and Girtin. A George Gross scene of Cockspur Street, London, the morning after an air raid, brought back vivid memories. Admiring a Rossetti drawing of Jane Morris (Mrs. William Morris), Eliot quoted from one of Rossetti's sonnets:

> *"Let all men note*
> *That in all years (O Love, thy gift is this!)*
> *They that would look on her must come to me."*

A Dali engraving of his study for the St. John of the Cross crucifixion drew a negative reaction. "I never feel anything when I look at a Dali," he commented, and although I couldn't agree with such a generalization, before I could say anything about it, Eliot's attention had turned to two enormous drawings by Eric Gill. They had attracted his attention, he said, when he had first entered the room. Framed in a single four-foot by six-foot oak frame with a burlap mat, they hung over the sofa on which he and my mother were seated. They were a representation of the two thieves that were hanged on either side of Christ at the Crucifixion. I told Eliot that an altarpiece for the Rossall School in Lancashire had been carved by Gill from these drawings. I also told him of my indebtedness to Bertram Rota, the eminent London bookseller, for getting them for me.

"I have never met Rota," Eliot said, "though, of course, he is well-known to me."

Commenting on Eric Gill, Eliot said, "Everything he has to say, everything he puts in a letter even, every work he puts his hand to, comes out of a completeness in himself. It is hardly a period in which we could have expected his like." Pausing for a moment, Eliot continued, "He is always unconventional, and so his undoubted orthodoxy always has great vitality. Pre-eminently, he shames us with the simplicity and directness of his acceptance of the Gospels."

"And his application of them to life?" I asked.

"Especially that gift," Eliot agreed, nodding his head several times.

After we all had a second drink, my mother announced that dinner was ready. On the way to the dining room, Eliot expressed interest in the entire apartment; therefore, while I assisted my mother in the kitchen, my father obligingly showed him around.

Eliot enjoyed the food tremendously. At the table my father talked with him about the shipping business, particularly with respect to English contracts during both wars. My mother spoke of her stamp collection and chanced to comment on the commemorative stamp picturing Whistler's Mother. Eliot said that he had been highly amused in his childhood by a painting of Whistler's Mother which parodied the original, showing the venerable lady standing up! This continued to amuse him inordinately, and was my first experience with Eliot's extremely droll sense of humor. I am certain that most of the stories that amused him found in him their only audience. For example, on two separate occasions he told me a favorite joke of his. It seems a boy was standing on the corner with his mouth open. A gentleman passing by stopped and said, "Better close your mouth, boy, or a fly will get in!" To which the boy replied, with his mouth still open—a trick of speech Eliot performed very convincingly: "Sir, that's why my mouth's open . . . the fly's in already and I'm waiting for him to get out!"

My mother said that she enjoyed detective and murder mysteries, particularly those of Dorothy Sayers. Eliot shared her enthusiasm: "I enjoy them, too, Mrs. Levy. They relax me enormously. My favorite is Agatha Christie. I believe she has the best-constructed plots, and no year passes without one or two appearing. I recommend *The Murder of Roger Ackroyd* if you have not read it."

Mother said she hadn't, but would on his recommendation. She thanked Eliot for his many letters, and he replied, "I am sorry, Mrs. Levy, that I cannot write to you in longhand. It may seem to be a rudeness, but I have developed a cramp in my hand and find that typing is much more comfortable for me."

After Eliot had finished his large dessert of peaches and ice cream, he looked down at his empty plate, and feigned astonishment by spreading both hands widely and exclaiming playfully, "There it isn't!" He told us he had often said that as a child, after a particularly good dessert.

I had never before seen Eliot in such good humor. He had, indeed, relaxed entirely and had made himself at home. I couldn't have been happier.

After dinner, in the living room, I excused myself, saying I had something to return to Eliot. He looked at me quizzically. I returned in a moment with a copy of the first American edition of *Nightwood* by Djuna Barnes, containing an introduction by Eliot. I handed it to him, saying, "I am happy to be able to return this to your library!"

Eliot put on his glasses, opened to the flyleaf of the book, and saw at once that it was his copy, inscribed to him by Djuna Barnes.

I said, "A colleague of mine picked this up for me in Paris."

Without a word, Eliot magisterially took out his fountain pen and wrote under Djuna Barnes's inscription, "I don't know how this got out of my possession: and I accuse no one. But now that it has found its way to William Turner Levy, it is in good hands and I want it to stay there. T. S. Eliot. 15.v.55."

"Isn't it odd that I never missed it?" he said.

"You probably lent it to someone and it got out of their hands," I conjectured.

[67]

"I am glad it didn't get back to Djuna—she's very sensitive! Aldous Huxley once wrote me an angry note because a bookseller's catalogue listed a book of his inscribed to me. I certainly did not sell it and thought it unkind of him to make that assumption."

We had arrived at my home at one-fifteen. It was now four o'clock and time to leave for a visit at the Niebuhrs', which I had arranged for Eliot.

After warm farewells to my parents, Eliot petted Judy, scratched her underneath the chin and said, "Well, Judy, I will hope to see you again." Judy rubbed up against his leg, expressing delight with the attention.

Outside, the cab I had ordered was waiting for us. On the way down the Henry Hudson Parkway, Eliot happened to notice a sign prohibiting funeral coaches from driving on the Parkway. The expression on Eliot's face showed his distress. His tone of voice was severe as he said: "Our attitude toward the dead shows what our values are. I'd call this shockingly disrespectful."

Eliot and I resumed our theological discussion. I recall two points that he made with pungency. The first was addressed directly to me:

"If you cannot reach your parishioners and touch their spirits in such a way that they want for themselves what God wants for them, you have not done your job. If it is only what you want, then even if they obey, it is just like obeying the law."

The second was a statement of his role as layman: "We, the lay people, must make the Church what it is. We, as well as the priests, have a responsibility. Let us suppose the Church is

[68]

closed by the state and attendance is on pain of death and the priest comes—and we are there! *We* must be there, *we* must bring *him* because our faith is *that real*."

We spoke briefly on Dom Gregory Dix, whose definitive work on the Eucharist I had just finished reading, and Eliot told me that he had met him when he had himself visited the Cowley Fathers, for whom he had a warm feeling. He also spoke of Ambrose Reeves, Bishop of South Africa, whose position against the state was adamant and outspoken. "He is a true Christian, and brave," Eliot concluded.

We then spoke in a desultory fashion of his recent visits to Majorca and Switzerland; and he next spoke of his pleasure in Harvard's President Pusey: "He has the charm of a John Keble."

Eliot's cat's name, I discovered, was Pettipaws, and apparently she had a very temperamental and expensive appetite. "Our housekeeper has her problems with Pettipaws! The previous cat I had, named Wiscus, was a fussy eater, too!" Mr. Eliot shared his Cheyne Walk apartment (shades of Carlyle and Henry James haunted the spot!) with John Hayward, a brilliant and distinguished figure in the London book world despite being confined to a wheelchair.

Eliot expressed deep concern over our current frustrations with the United Nations, but hoped the organization could somehow be strengthened.

I touched on American politics and Eliot said, "I never enter into such discussions any more because I am not well enough informed, although I follow all the news with close interest. I like both Stevenson and Eisenhower as men and I rejoice that America is so fortunate. I do not know the issues, really, but I suppose that if I were an American I would be more attracted to Stevenson."

He started to tell me about the impressive service he had attended in Washington on Ascension Day when we pulled up in front of the Niebuhrs'. He stepped out as I paid the cab driver, who said, "I feel I ought not to charge you—he's so interesting!"

We found Reinhold Niebuhr in good spirits and with sufficient energy to enjoy the visit. We settled comfortably and Mrs. Niebuhr served tea.

During our conversation Niebuhr mentioned, deprecatingly, the ego of cats, and Eliot responded gently by saying that he once stayed for a weekend in a house with Yorkshire terriers, and reached the conclusion that he couldn't work with a dog in the house!

Both touched on the unfortunate decline of language into jargon. Concerning philosophers, Niebuhr felt that it would end with them just "talking to themselves," and Eliot sadly agreed, saying, "That, of course, is the death of philosophy."

"You had Bertrand Russell as a teacher, didn't you?" Niebuhr asked Eliot.

"Oh, yes," Eliot answered, "he said at the time I was one of his most promising students. He was in for a disappointment!"

Niebuhr referred to Sir Harold Laski. "Remember," he said, "fifteen years ago he *was* the London School of Economics—now, there are 'none so poor as to do him reverence.'"

Both men shook their heads in a silent, sad recognition of human ingratitude and public restlessness in search for the new.

Niebuhr and I talked of *Moby Dick*. He felt that Melville

had been influenced by Augustine in his concept of the whiteness of the whale. I was pleased that Niebuhr was so impressed with the book, which I consider the best written by an American. Eliot threw cold water on our joint enthusiasm: "I am not keen on Melville, never have been." In reply to my query, he added, "No, I have never read 'Benito Cereno.' "

There was talk of W. H. Auden ("Wystan" to the Niebuhrs) and of Enid Starkie, Professor of Poetry at Oxford, whom Niebuhr quoted a friend as calling a "formidable woman, with Irish chin stuck out—no stopping her!"

Niebuhr spoke of the touch of fanaticism in Toynbee, whom Eliot also found wanting, and of Herbert Butterfield's failure, as a historian, to see gradations in sin. Both men spoke of Anthony Eden, using the adjectives "pale" and "anemic." Eden, in the shadow of Churchill, had promised much, and both Eliot and Niebuhr shared the general disappointment in Eden's inability to rise to the demands of top leadership. This led Niebuhr to relate a story he was told by someone who had supposedly heard Churchill tell it: "The trouble with America," the Prime Minister had said, "is that she has gone from barbarism to decadence without having passed through civilization!" Eliot was distressed by the flippancy, and said so. There was a momentary exchange on the lapses of great men.

When it was time to depart, Mrs. Niebuhr asked the overcoated Eliot to step into a bathroom to see a newly acquired French poodle.

"Just a puppy, Mr. Eliot. I wonder if you would do us the honor of naming it."

The author of "The Naming of Cats" took it as a serious

matter, and replied that if it were a cat he might consider it, but that he felt utterly unable to name a dog. I felt that Eliot not only honestly admitted his singular affection for cats, but also honored the dog by not belittling it with a name chosen perfunctorily.

On the way back to Mr. Giroux's apartment, I told Eliot that Niebuhr had some time ago mentioned to me that he used the *Four Quartets* again and again as devotional reading. Eliot replied, "He honors me with his humility."

Before we parted, Eliot said, "Thank you for taking such good care of me and making everything so pleasant and easy. I sail on the *Queen Mary* a month from today—do call me on the fourteenth of June, when I return from Cambridge, and perhaps we can arrange to see each other."

I next saw Eliot aboard the *Queen Mary* on June 15. I was waiting alone in his stateroom when he entered at three o'clock that afternoon. In what seemed like a single movement, he shook my hand, flung himself into an armchair, dropped his worn briefcase on the floor at his side and unbuttoned his overcoat.

I presented him with a book I knew he wanted to read, Sir Thomas Browne's *Christian Morals*.

Eliot said, "I am familiar, of course, with Browne's better-known work, *Religio Medici,* but I had never heard of this one before you mentioned it at our last meeting."

He opened the book, flipped a few pages and noticed my name on the flyleaf. "I see that it is your copy."

"It's out of print," I responded, "and I didn't want you to have to wait to read it. I'll get another copy."

"I shall read your marked copy with all the more interest,"

he replied, "and I will return it to you the next time we meet. You may, then, if you like, order me a copy. I recall your saying that it was a favorite of Samuel Johnson's, and that is a further strong recommendation."

Eliot and I walked out onto the deck into the pleasant sunlight. "I wish I'd brought a camera," I said.

"I am just as happy you didn't, William. I do not object to being photographed, but I do not like it—it seems a disruption of whatever you are doing, a distraction."

I confessed that I felt the same way.

Eliot continued, "But I will arrange for you to have a photograph, if you like." He did not forget.

A clanging gong announced to all visitors that it was time for them to disembark. I turned to Eliot, handed him a folded typed sheet of paper and said, "I think you'd like to see this. It's the Invocation I'm delivering tonight at the City College Commencement."

Eliot took the paper and put it in his inside breast pocket. "At what time will you deliver this?"

"At eight-thirty," I answered.

"Good! I will read it at that time precisely—and I will think of you."

That evening at the time I delivered the Invocation, *I* was thinking of *Eliot*.

# Chapter Seven

Two weeks later, back in London, Eliot wrote me:

"I had a comfortable journey with no difficulties of transport at the end. The restfulness of the voyage was impaired only by the number of people who seemed to want to make my acquaintance for one reason or another, including a young lady who appeared to consider that the fact that she knew a certain Mr. Tyrone Power (who is, I believe, a film actor) entitled her to my acquaintance also."

In the same letter, Eliot commented on remarks I had written him concerning Roosevelt and Churchill when they were in conference together at Casablanca during the war. F.D.R. was concerned with the poverty-stricken population, making plans to ameliorate their plight when he returned to private life; whereas Churchill betook himself to the oasis at Marrakesh to paint!

"I have been re-reading your letter of June 9th. I don't wish to discourage in the least your researches into the late Mr.

Roosevelt's Christianity and churchmanship [I had started writing a book on Roosevelt's religion], but I wonder whether his attempt, as you say, to educate Churchill in 'the brotherhood of man' is so indicative of his spiritual superiority as would appear. It may have been simply a difference in experience and vocabulary. I confess that if I found myself for business reasons in a country the poverty of which I was not at that moment in a position to mitigate, I should think that I would be well employed in the intervals of business in painting a desert sunset."

I had known Eleanor Roosevelt as a friend for several years. After I had spent a long weekend at Hyde Park, I wrote Eliot that Mrs. Roosevelt and I had gone swimming together every day. Unable to imagine the aristocratic-looking former First Lady (at approximately his own age) diving into a pool, Eliot felt sure that he had misread my letter. He wrote:

"I interpreted one sentence at first as stating that Mrs. Roosevelt went in swimming with you once or twice every day, but a second reading makes me think that, perhaps it was only you that swam, and that Mrs. Roosevelt merely dined."

Eliot and Franklin D. Roosevelt had something in common. Having entered Harvard two years after Roosevelt's graduation, Eliot became an editor of the *Harvard Advocate,* of which F.D.R. had been editor-in-chief. I wrote Eliot about an editorial Roosevelt had written protesting the perfunctory religious services at the Chapel. Eliot replied, in the same letter: "It is interesting that Roosevelt as a Harvard undergraduate and as an undergraduate journalist, protested against the Chapel services. He would, I think, be gratified by the improvements initiated by President Pusey."

A few months later, Eliot sent me a presentation copy of the address, *Goethe as the Sage,* which he had delivered in Hamburg at the time he was awarded the Hanseatic Goethe Prize.

Judy, the cat Eliot had met at my home, died in October of 1955. I communicated this to Eliot, but was able to add the good news that we had acquired a kitten, which my mother had named Lord Peter Wimsey after the detective hero in Dorothy Sayers's mystery novels. Eliot wrote:

"I condole with you on the death of your Cat and rejoice with you over the acquisition of a male successor. I have always held that the best cats were likely to be of obscure origin. Pedigree cats are no good, stupid, nervous and of feeble character. The common cat, on the other hand, is either good or bad, but is apt to be a cat of strong character, whether for good or evil."

That Christmas I sent Eliot three ornamental wire cats: one, a planter, another, a magazine rack, and the third, a letter holder. He replied:

"I am tardy in writing to you, as the first Cats arrived well before Christmas. It has, so to speak, been raining Cats but I am happy to say not Dogs. Now that the shower is over—and I warn you, there isn't room in this apartment for MORE cats—I can write to express my appreciation of these remarkable felines—two of them Practical and the third (the copper one) has been converted to Practicality, as my housekeeper is now training a climbing house plant to grow in and out of him. I doubt whether Pettipaws, who dominates this establishment and whose insistence on eating nothing but rabbit is going to bring us to penury, has sufficiently developed her powers of abstraction to recognise her features in those of these amiable animals.

"Anyway, I am appreciative, if she is not."

Eliot was coming to America again! He wrote on April 14, 1956:

"I shall hope to see you before long. I shall be but briefly in New York, and alas, my schedule seems to deposit me everywhere else of a Sunday: Minneapolis, Chicago, Washington and Boston. But I shall telephone and trust we can arrange a meeting—if not on my first passage through New York, on my second or third return. I sail on the Q Mary on the 19th."

This time in America, at the University of Minnesota, Eliot would lecture to the largest audience any literary figure had ever appeared before, and for it he would receive the largest fee ever paid.

# Chapter Eight

"This is the first springlike day we've had—it must be in honor of your arrival!" I said.

"No, no. It's St. Mark's feast day!" Eliot responded.

It was April 25, 1956, and we were in a cab on our way to my home again, this time for lunch.

"Here is your book, William," Eliot said as he returned my copy of *Christian Morals*.

"Would you like to keep it, or have me get you a copy?"

"No, thank you. After I read it I found I could easily get a copy in London and did so to save you the trouble. I marked several passages to point out to you."

Eliot put on his glasses and read aloud two passages, one referring to ancient Greece and Rome and how a lesson could be learned through the example of ethics and morality that flourished at that ancient time; the other illustrating how a crucial moral point could be exemplified in the most humble and simple life.

Somehow our conversation led to the disappointment felt on both sides of the Atlantic in Prime Minister Anthony Eden's conduct of affairs. "He is not in good health," Eliot proclaimed, "he has no verve." Eliot went on to say that he had admired Eden very much at the time of the Munich crisis. "His resignation from the Chamberlain cabinet then was an eloquent act. I felt a deep personal guilt and shame for my country and for myself as a part of the country. Our whole national life seemed fraudulent. If our culture led to an act of betrayal of that kind, then such a culture was worthless, worthless because it was bankrupt. It had no morality because it did not finally believe in anything."

I was seeing an Eliot I had never seen before, the man who felt passionately enough about public behavior to write *Notes Toward the Definition of Culture* and *The Idea of a Christian Society*. His chagrin was still acute fifteen years after Munich.

"We were concerned with safety, with our possessions, with money, not with right and wrong. We had forgot Goethe's advice: 'The dangers of life are infinite and *safety* is among them.'

"The systems we put together without regard to man's nature must fall apart. Today I think of the Church biding its time, speaking out the truth, but waiting until people turn and listen again. Not a pleasant prospect before us, is it?" Eliot concluded with a sad smile. "And it does not improve matters that the Church's ministry simply is not able to attract the best minds any longer."

Suddenly he looked at me seriously and said he wished I lived in London. "I would like to see a young man like you rector of our parish!"

[79]

At this very moment we arrived in front of my apartment house.

On the way in, Eliot noticed purple irises blooming against the red brick wall of the house. He remembered, "They were in bloom the last time I was here."

I was reminded of Eliot's fear of self-service elevators. He breathed an audible sigh of relief as we exited on the eleventh floor. Eliot turned to his right and asked, "This is the way, isn't it?" I told him that it was, flattered that he should remember.

My father was not able to be at home on this occasion. My mother answered the door. Eliot shook her hand, kissed her, and said, "I'm in no hurry today, I'm thankful to say."

Mother stepped aside and Eliot saw our new cat coming to greet him. Eliot removed his coat and handed it to me along with his hat. His attention went to the cat. He stooped down and said, "Lord Peter Wimsey, I'm your Uncle Possum!" Wimsey, usually aloof with strangers, purred loudly and rubbed up against his legs.

We all had champagne before lunch. Eliot asked if he might smoke. It was the first time I saw him smoke a cigar. It was a long Havana, which he unwrapped carefully and lit with his own cigarette lighter. He leaned back and said, "My doctor had me stop smoking cigarettes, but I have a cigar from time to time. They are prohibitively expensive in England, however. Smoking a cigar makes me feel so distinguished and European—like Thomas Mann!" he added with a broad smile.

Mother served black olives with our drink, remembering that Eliot had liked them the last time. "Something I do not get at home," he commented appreciatively.

I mentioned that colleagues and students of mine would from time to time ask me if Eliot was anti-Semitic, sometimes just assuming that he was. Eliot agreed completely with my way of handling such questions. First, by asking what evidence there was, and then by examining and evaluating the line of prose or verse which appeared to them to have such a connotation. "I am grieved and sometimes angered by this matter," Eliot added. "I am not an anti-Semite and never have been. It seems to me unfortunate that persons give that odious term such a broad and ill-defined definition. American Jews are sensitive in a way you never find is true of their counterparts in England, although I can realize that there are several reasons for this."

I asked him if he ever replied to such attacks. "I do if the attack is responsible and sober."

Eliot added, "It is a terrible slander on a man. And they do not know, as you and I do, that in the eyes of the Church, to be anti-Semitic is a sin."

I asked if he ever received similar attacks from the Irish, who could also point to unflattering references that Eliot had made to them, in his early poems. "No, and I have two close friends whose names are Sweeney!"

I asked Eliot if he had ever heard the recording of his poems from *Old Possum's Book of Practical Cats* as read by Robert Donat with music by Alan Rawsthorne. He said that he had heard some of them in a rehearsal, but not the final recording, and would be interested to hear one or two of the poems. So, after lunch, I played "The Naming of Cats" and "Macavity: the Mystery Cat" for him. His reaction was favorable. "I like the idea that they are read against the musical background and not themselves set to the music," he said, "but I am not at all sure yet what I think of it, and, of course, I should have to hear them all."

He mentioned, in passing, that he liked *Peter and the Wolf,* and when I told him that Mrs. Roosevelt had done the narration in a recent recording, he showed such genuine interest that I promised to send him the record.

I asked him about the recordings he had done of the *Four Quartets* for the British Arts Council. "They were very difficult to do, William, and we recorded them over and over again, painstakingly. Sometimes it would be just right, I thought, and then we would discover a slight background noise, like the rustle of the turning of a page!"

This conversation led me to ask him if he would be willing to read the third Quartet, "The Dry Salvages," aloud. I told him that it meant more to me than any other poem.

"You will have to provide me with a copy," he said. "I would not trust my memory." I did, and later, back in my room, Eliot read the third Quartet.

I showed him a photographic reproduction of an early drawing of himself by Wyndham Lewis, one of a small number that were made and that he had signed at the time.

Eliot said, "The painting Lewis did from this and other studies hangs by the staircase in the Hall at Magdalene College, Cambridge. I will send you a snapshot of it and a postcard of the Hall. The painting is perfectly placed to keep it from being seen," he laughed. "It is poorly lighted and there is almost no place to stand where you can get far enough away from it to see it properly."

I asked Eliot if he thought the likeness was a good one.

"I think it a very creditable likeness—in so far as I can recall what I looked like then!"

I had been fortunate in acquiring a pencil portrait of Eliot done by his sister-in-law, Theresa G. Eliot. I had it matted in blue and framed in gold with a small overhead light attached to the frame. When I pointed it out to Eliot, he said, not unkindly, "Ah, I see you have one of the corpse drawings!" When I looked puzzled, he hastened to explain himself. "Theresa wanted me to sit, but I could not find the time, so one afternoon she did a series of them while I was stretched out on the sofa for a nap. Naturally, in most of them, my eyes are closed—though not in this one—so I call them the corpse drawings!"

When we sat down to lunch, I asked Eliot if he would please say grace. He consented, and used the Latin grace of Magdalene College, Cambridge, of which he was an Honorary Fellow.

Later, I asked him if he would send me a copy of the prayer for my own use.

"I will write it out for you while I am here," he said, sitting down at my desk. He wrote the following, which I later preserved in a Hogarth frame with a black-and-gold mat painted on the glass:

> *Benedic Domine et his donis tuis*
> *quae de tua largitate sumus*
> *sumpturi; et concede ut illis*
> *salubriter nutriti tibi debitum*
> *obsequium praestare valeamus,*
> *per Jesum Christum dominum*
> *nostrum.   Amen.*

A loose translation would be:

> *Bless us, O Lord, and bless thy gifts*
> *which we are about to receive of thy bounty—*

*and grant that, sustained thereby in body,*
*we may be strengthened to offer*
*that spiritual service which is due to thee.*
*Through Jesus Christ our Lord.   Amen.*

I saw Eliot back to Robert Giroux's apartment, where he was staying once again. Before we parted, Eliot said, "I will be traveling extensively in America now, but I will be back in New York a day or so before I sail on June sixth. Could you see me off then, and also perhaps arrange another meeting with Niebuhr? I would like to see him before I leave because you tell me his health is failing."

On the evening of June 4, I was delighted when I answered the telephone and heard Eliot's voice.

"William?"

"Welcome back to New York, Mr. Eliot."

"Thank you, William. Frankly, I look forward to getting aboard the *Queen Mary*. I have had a very exhausting time."

I realized that his voice was unsteady.

"Can't you take it easy until then? Are there things you simply have to do?" I asked.

"I am afraid there are a few obligations. But one thing I want to do is see Niebuhr. Could you pick me up tomorrow at four if Niebuhr could receive us at four-thirty?"

"Of course," I said, anxious to terminate the conversation and give him an opportunity to rest, adding gently, "I'll ring your bell at four. If Niebuhr isn't free, and then only, I'll call you back."

"You are very good, William. I have so much to tell you—I lectured on criticism to an audience of fifteen thousand in Minneapolis—if you can picture that!"

"If you need me, please call. I'll be home all evening."

"No need, William, I will be all right. But it is reassuring to know you are so near."

The next afternoon, I found Eliot looking tired, but well, and in good spirits. I did notice, however, that he walked more slowly than usual.

"We pass the Cathedral of St. John the Divine on our way uptown," I said. "If you'd like five minutes inside I can have the cab wait. And we can also fit in Grant's Tomb, which you had mentioned wanting to see. But neither is important, unless you really want to see them."

"By all means let us stop—if we have the time."

When we entered the cathedral, Eliot remembered that it was here that I had been ordained. I showed him the magnificent stained-glass windows and we toured the chapels behind the high altar. He spoke sadly of the fact that we saw only one other person there, a verger. "These cathedrals—and I speak of ours in England, too—re-echo in their emptiness." Several years later, when he sent me his essay, *The Value and Use of Cathedrals in England Today,* I remembered this moment.

Eliot enjoyed our brief stop at Grant's Tomb. I told him that as a boy my father had, like other school children, contributed one cent to the tomb's construction.

"That gives you a warm feeling towards it, I am sure," he said. "It is a very special feeling to have contributed to the creation of something that lasts."

Inside, he was particularly interested in the flags of various Civil War regiments and in photographs. It was a past in which his family had had an honorable part.

Eliot said, "I think of Mark Twain very kindly in connection with the publishing of Grant's memoirs [he pronounced the word in the British manner—"meemoirs"]. It was a generous act."

Eliot, I observed, always credited courage and generosity very highly. He had said to me once, "I agree with Dr. Johnson when he says that courage is the greatest of the virtues, for without it we can practice no other."

The tea with Reinhold Niebuhr was quiet, pleasant, and serious. I recall only one remark of Eliot's. He quoted Simone Weil when speaking of what each of us owes to his country: "She puts it, I feel, very well: 'The state should not require that we give everything always, but that we should give everything sometimes.'" I also recall an intrusive feeling that this would be the last time the two men would meet.

When I returned with Eliot to the apartment where he was staying, I said, "Can I help you get to the ship tomorrow?"

"No, thank you," he said, "that has all been arranged, but I will expect to see you there at one-thirty, and do bring your mother if she would like to come. I assume your father will be at work."

"My mother and I will be there," I said.

Noticing the worried look on my face, he added, "Good night, William. Do not worry. I will get to bed early tonight and sleep late tomorrow."

I am certain he did just that, but when my mother and I saw him the following afternoon, he still looked unwell.

We spoke briefly. He admired the flowers my mother had brought. He was breathing heavily.

"Wouldn't it be better if we ran along," I asked; "then you could rest a bit?"

"I think that would be wise," he replied. He kissed my mother good-by, solemnly shook my hand, and accepted a gift from me which I suggested he open later.

As I closed the cabin door, I saw that Eliot was already seated on the bed, pulling off his jacket and vest.

# Chapter Nine

## EXHAUSTED T. S. ELIOT
## RUSHED TO HOSPITAL

*Taken Off Liner;*
*American Trip*
*Wearies Poet*

London, June 12 [1956] (By the United Press). Poet-playwright
T. S. Eliot, exhausted by a six-week visit to his native United
States, was taken by ambulance from the liner Queen Mary to a
hospital today, suffering an abnormally rapid heartbeat.

The 67-year-old Nobel Prize winner was stricken two days outside New York on the voyage back from his trip to America. He
has been afflicted for some time with an abnormally rapid heartbeat, known medically as tachycardia.

Ship officials said Mr. Eliot made the last half of the crossing in
sick bay.

When the ship reached Southampton, he was taken ashore, pale
but smiling, by wheelchair and put into an ambulance.

At the French Hospital in London, a spokesman said Mr. Eliot was "much better."

I was shocked to read this news report at breakfast, just one week after seeing Eliot off on the *Queen Mary*. Before I left the house that morning, I wrote him a brief note and sent it air mail. Later my parents and I sent flowers and wrote additional notes. When I didn't hear from him by June 29, I telephoned him at his home in London.

When I heard his voice, I asked, "Is everything all right?"

"How good of you to call, William. This is the first telephone call I have ever had from America. Yes, I am fine, really. The newspaper reports were much exaggerated. I think it providential that the attack occurred after I had boarded the ship. It would have been a dreadful nuisance to be hospitalized in New York, though of course you would have been there. The flowers were abundant and so lovely. After enjoying them, I sent them to the chapel altar. And do thank the Sisters for having remembered me at the altar." (I had prayers said for Eliot by the nuns at the House of the Redeemer, an Episcopal retreat house in New York.)

After talking to my mother, he told me: "I can visualize you both at the telephone in your study. My New England conscience makes me fear that you are spending too much on me to be talking at such length. I must write a letter soon. There is a lot of mail to be taken care of, but yours has a high priority!"

Then Eliot asked me, "Is Wimsey right there?"

I told him he was and that he was fine.

"Well, take good care of *yourself,* William. Good-by, good-by."

Three days later, on July 2, 1956, Eliot wrote me the following letter:

"I have much for which to thank you: lunch at the family apartment, the visit to the Niebuhrs, you and your mother coming to see me off (I was not at my best, as the tachycardia had begun half an hour before I saw you!), your present, your messages to the hospital and since, the superb sheaf of mixed spring and summer flowers, and finally your telephone call—a compliment which no one has ever before paid me: only once before have I had a transatlantic call, and that was only a quite superfluous business request.

"And it was a great pleasure to see you so well, and apparently so happy in your work.

"I was pleased to get your lovely K'ang postcards (it is exasperating that I never have the *time,* on these visits, to get to the museums)."

I had discovered that Eliot was particularly fond of Chinese vases and porcelains, when he admired a piece which I possessed. I suggested taking him to New York's Metropolitan Museum of Art to see their extensive collection, but as there wasn't time to do so, sent him a set of colored postcard reproductions instead.

"As for Rougemont's book [*Love in the Western World*] it was first published in English by Faber & Faber. I trust what you read was the new edition, which the author has altered and expanded, and which I have not myself examined.

"'The Family Reunion' has had two previous productions in London, in 1939 and in 1947; but this production is said to be especially brilliant, and I am going to see it shortly. My illness, by the way, was briefer than any of my previous attacks of the same ailment, and I am almost fully active again.

[*90*]

"Now about the Roosevelt plate [the gift I had given him aboard the *Queen Mary:* a dinner plate that had been used at Hyde Park in F.D.R.'s time, bearing the initials of the President's father, James Roosevelt—a rare and historical item. I had enclosed a letter explaining its history] —a subject which I approach with hesitation and misgiving, and only after much thought. The natives of Western Africa, I am told, when they give a present to anyone they hold in esteem and in warm friendship, choose only as a gift something that they themselves covet or cherish. This, my dear William, is what you have done: I know your admiration for Franklin Roosevelt and your friendship for his widow; and I appreciate what it means that you should give me something which has so much symbolic value to yourself. Now I do not know what attitude on the part of the recipient of such a gift is considered proper in West Africa, but I know what attitude my own conscience dictates. That is, that the recipient should only accept the gift if it has the same significance for him as it has for the giver: otherwise, he is unworthy of it.

"For I am afraid I cannot look at the late Franklin Roosevelt with your eyes. I do not impugn his character or his motives. And I have long since ceased to take sides in American party politics—I respect the achievements of Harry Truman and those of Dwight Eisenhower. Nor do I overlook the great generosity of Lend Lease; or am I mindless of what the outcome of the war would have been, for England, if America had taken no part in it. But what I also cannot forget is that Mr. Roosevelt was no great friend of England; that he was suspicious of British policy and disapproving of the existence of the (now almost inexistent) British Empire. Oh my dear William, the harm that has been done in the world, the dis-

[*91*]

order that is only now too evident, by the ju-ju of those words 'colonialism' and imperialism' working in American breasts! Was it this perhaps that led Mr. Roosevelt to embark on the disastrous policy of agreeing with Stalin rather than with Churchill, or surrendering position after position to the Kremlin? Anyway, I regard Mr. Roosevelt's foreign policy as a colossal folly which opened the way towards the Dark Ages to which the world seems to me to be advancing.

"Feeling as I do, will you forgive me for regarding it as my duty to restore the plate to your hands on our next meeting? Nothing would please me more as a token of your tolerance, than the gift, when I return this plate, of a plate—a kitchen plate—Wimsey's plate—from the Levy household for which I am always glad to pray. God bless you."

Although I was shocked to learn Eliot's view of certain aspects of Roosevelt's foreign policy, I appreciated the elaborate, almost ceremonial nature of the refusal which he had not just written as a letter, but "composed" as an essay. I was flattered by his concern for my feelings, and at the same time respected his character as revealed in his unwillingness to accept the object, and thus not mislead me as to his attitude. Consequently, I wrote and told him that although I disagreed with his view of history, I thought it not only reasonable but even desirable that good friends should disagree. Public issues ought not to decide personal affections.

I was pleased to learn in his next letter, dated August 4, 1956, that I had made my feelings clear:

"I was immensely relieved to get your letter of the 30th July. My letter had not been easy to write; and in spite of all efforts, I feared that you might be wounded. Your reply could not be better worded or more generously inspired.

"I am now recovered and fully active—that is to say, as active as is reasonable at my age—and leaving for a month's holiday in Switzerland on the 14th. I am sorry to learn that your holiday is to be so brief. [I had written to Eliot that I was going to Arlington, Vermont, for two weeks.] Two weeks is not enough for a person who has responsibilities and therefore nervous wear and tear. When I was 30, I got two weeks holiday a year, but a little later, when I was advanced to three weeks, I realised that that third week made a lot of difference. Two weeks for rest, after which a week for enjoyment and positive improvement of health.

"I don't see how Milton comes into a series on Anglicanism and Literature—but you seem to be in good company. Rosamund Tuve wrote an interesting book on George Herbert. I ought to have said, that it is I who find myself in good company!"

The latter was a reference to an invitation to me from the Dean and Chapter of the Cathedral of St. John the Divine in New York to lecture on Eliot in the spring before a Sunday evening seminar of faculty and students. Two other speakers had been invited to lecture on Milton and Herbert, respectively.

I sent Eliot a birthday prayer and a letter, which included a cheerful report on my father's health. From this time on, I would keep him informed of my father's up-and-down, but slowly and steadily deteriorating state of health. He answered on September 28:

"I was happy to get your letter 'for the 26th September', and to know that your father was feeling much better. I shall hope to have still better news of him later.

"Meanwhile I have to thank your mother for her birthday

card (which arrived just before the date) and you for two gifts. The Last Supper of Dali [a print which I had acquired in Washington] is very interesting indeed: I shan't know whether I like it until I have looked at it again and again—and I was much interested to learn that the painter (which I did not know) had repudiated his early doctrines and returned to the fold. Also for the Hanged Man [a card from a French 1720 Tarot deck. In *The Waste Land* Eliot referred to the hanged man] (who seems to accept so philosophically his uncomfortable position): but I am sorry to hear that The Waste Land has caused the rifling of Tarot Packs. Still, the use of such cards for divination is certainly a black art forbidden to the faithful.

"I'm glad to hear you found the trip to Washington profitable, especially as you had such a brief visit to Arlington this year. I enjoy visiting my friends in Washington, and the city is impressive (the Episcopal Cathedral, though unfinished, is magnificent); but I have always said that it was an impossible place to live in except for politicians, diplomats, civil servants and newspaper folk.

"My holiday in Switzerland was a damp one—I have never experienced so much rain there at this time of year, and sometimes torrential for long periods—crops ruined—weather cold —but I enjoyed as always being with my oldest friends. Now I am settling down for the winter."

Eliot wrote me only one longhand letter in all the years we corresponded. I felt that it was a deliberate decision on his part, prompted by a concern for my father's health coupled with the fact that he had not heard from me for some time. It was dated November 13, 1956:

[94]

"I have not heard from you for a long time. I hope this does not mean illness & anxiety in your household. Do let me have a line to let me know how your father is. My love and sympathy—& prayers—we need yours too!"

13 Nov. 1956.

My dear William

I have not heard from you for along time. I hope this does not mean illness & anxiety in your household. Do let me have a line to let me know how your father is. My love & sympathy - & prayers - we need yours too!

Affectionately

T. S. Eliot

Eliot had been correct. My temporary silence had been imposed by my father's health, which had suffered a severe, though temporary, setback. I wrote to him at once to relieve his anxiety, and he replied on November 21:

"I am writing to acknowledge your letter of the 17th, received this morning, and to give you and your mother my warm sympathy. I shall certainly remember you all in my prayers. I know of another case of hardening of the arteries, and I know that the most painful aspect of this for relatives, is the apparent change of character and the appearance of unreasonable and often disagreeable traits of character. One has always to remember that this is the result of a physical cause breaking the communication of the real person with the world, and continue to see the beloved person apart from manifestations which are not in character. I am sure that this situation is a great strain for all of you, and I hope that your being immersed in such congenial and valuable work helps you to bear this misfortune."

On Christmas Day, Eliot wrote a letter addressed to "Florence, Jack, William & Wimsey":

"My Christmas Greetings to you to-day, and grateful thanks for the parcel which has now been opened and disclosed the good Cheese and no end of Devilled Ham. And for your Christmas Card and for keeping me in your kind thoughts.

"Devilled Ham is still packed in the same little cans with the same label as in my childhood, when it was the staple content for the food baskets that my family took when we made our annual journey in June from St. Louis to Boston. There were not always restaurant cars in those days (when the Pullman sleepers were lit by gas) and the family occupied a 'stateroom' and two upper-and-lowers. (I felt very grown up when I was first allowed to sleep in an upper berth).

"I hope that William will always continue to keep me informed about himself and his family, whose friendship means a great deal to their friend."

Eliot signed the letter, as usual, "T. S. Eliot," but then in parentheses, "or Tom." It had never seemed, in all the years of our friendship, uncomfortable for me to call so formal a man as T. S. Eliot, "Mr. Eliot." Now he had decided that I should call him "Tom." I soon found it just as comfortable. From this date on, all of his letters to me were signed "Tom."

I had read once that T. S. Eliot was known as Tom to a circle of the smallest possible radius. I now considered my admission to that select circle a priceless Christmas gift.

# Chapter Ten

### T. S. ELIOT, 68, MARRIES HIS SECRETARY, 30

LONDON, Jan. 10 [1957] (UP). Nobel Prize winning poet T. S. Eliot quietly married his secretary today.

The sixty-eight-year-old American-born poet took Valerie Fletcher as his second wife in a pre-dawn ceremony attended only by a few friends and the bride's parents.

The bride, about thirty, was Mr. Eliot's private secretary at the publishing firm of Faber and Faber. They had been close friends for a long time, but the wedding came as a surprise.

Mr. Eliot won the Nobel Prize for Literature in 1948, a year after the death of his first wife.

Tom wrote me: "It is a wonderful thing, my dear William, to be happily married, and a very blessed state for those who are called to it, even at my age. I have a very beautiful and good and sensitive wife, with a very good mind as well and a passionate love of poetry—she has everything to make me happy, and I am humbly thankful."

As a wedding present, I wanted to give the Eliots something American, preferably something antique. I decided on a large square of linen that had been block printed about a hundred and fifty years ago with a scene depicting William Penn trading with Indians. I had purchased it some years earlier from the estate of a family in Arlington, Vermont; it had been part of a drapery. Examples of this kind of work are now usually found only in museums.

Rather than have it framed in New York and then crated, I delegated the task of framing to my bookseller friend Bertram Rota in London. He took great pains in finding a handsome, mottled cherrywood frame of the same period, and had the print stretched and matted with burlap. I told him he could invite the Eliots to inspect it, rather than merely deliver it, for Tom had more than once expressed a desire to meet Rota.

Tom acknowledged the gift in his letter dated May 18, 1957:

"As we had been invited by Mr. Rota to come in for a drink on the occasion of receiving your present, and could not for some days find a convenient time, we were slow in receiving it. Then I did not want to write to thank you for it until we had decided on the place to hang it in; and that was not finally decided until last night, when a small hanging committee consisting of Valerie and myself and her parents came to a conclusion and hung the picture. It is at the end of the corridor and is therefore the first object that a visitor is likely to notice when the front door is opened. It's a fascinating picture in itself, apart from its historical interest, and by the way is beautifully and most suitably framed. So you see, the gift is appreciated and will serve as a constant daily reminder of the giver. We both want to thank you very much indeed."

The time came for me to deliver the lecture at The Cathedral of St. John the Divine. I entitled it "The Idea of the Church in T. S. Eliot." It was well received and there was the suggestion that either the National Council of the Protestant Episcopal Church or *The Christian Scholar,* a quarterly, would want to print it. Before submitting it, I wanted Tom's approval. He wrote on June 22:

"I have gone through your lecture once with pleasure and a general feeling of warm approval. If anything, what you say is, as I had feared it might be, too complimentary to my work. I shall read it again however with a view to discovering whether I have any criticisms of value to make. I have no objection to your National Council going ahead with it."

The lecture was printed by *The Christian Scholar,* and I sent several copies to Tom. He told me when I saw him next that it was the best thing that had ever been written about his religious beliefs, and urged me to expand it into a book. "Prior to your work, all I received was abusive criticism. There was no attempt to understand and define my position. I cannot tell you how grateful I am that this is now available."

Tom sent me his new book *On Poetry and Poets,* a collection of essays, as well as his Minneapolis lecture, now separately printed as *The Frontiers of Criticism,* and a copy of the Penguin *Selected Prose,* which he had noticed was missing from my collection of his works.

Tom wrote: "I managed to finish off the first draft of the play on which I have been working [*The Elder Statesman*]

[*100*]

—its future is still uncertain, and I never yield to the persuasion to be sure that a play of mine is to be produced, until the curtain goes up on the first act. I can only say that it is a very different play (and I believe a better one) for so much of it having been written during this last year, than it would have been if I had finished it before our marriage."

Tom added, "We celebrated our first wedding anniversary yesterday by going to see 'The Tempest'—an interesting production, but John Gielgud very disappointing, according to our notions of Prospero."

I had sent them an anniversary card and Tom responded: "It's wonderful that you should remember the date, delightful that you should send us a card of congratulation and good wishes, and miraculous that it should have arrived on the very day. Thank you from both of us!"

In March of 1958, Tom wrote me of his and Valerie's impending visit to America. They would arrive on April 19 and have two nights in New York before going to the University of Texas, where Tom was to give a poetry reading. Then they were scheduled to return to New York for another poetry reading at Columbia University. After this they planned to spend three weeks in Cambridge before sailing back to England from New York.

At both universities, Tom would be paid astronomical fees.

On the night of his arrival, I called Tom at the apartment of Margie Cohn (widow of Louis H. Cohn), a distinguished New York bookseller, owner of House of Books, Ltd., where he and Valerie were staying. When I greeted him, he said, "This is the first time I have heard you call me Tom, and I must say it sounds very well!" I told him that I was pleased and flattered to do so. At the conclusion of our conversation, he said, "I am most anxious to have you meet my beautiful wife!"

We had arranged to see each other on Sunday, April 27, after his return from Texas.

## Chapter Eleven

When I saw Tom he was wearing a ten-gallon hat and carrying an umbrella. We were going to church!

"This hat was given to me in Texas," Tom said proudly, as he, Valerie, my parents and I rode in the family car to All Angels' Church.

After the service, we all went to my home for Sunday dinner.

"Dear," Tom said to Valerie, "I should like to introduce Lord Peter Wimsey!" Wimsey was just as gracious in making the acquaintance of Mrs. Eliot as he had been in meeting her husband.

As we entered my study, Tom pointed out the view of the Hudson to his new wife.

"It's all exactly the way Tom described it to me," Valerie said with a charming smile. "I'm so pleased to be here."

After everyone had taken seats in my study, I brought in a

bottle of champagne and was surprised to hear Tom say, with a glint in his eye, "I'll have a very dry martini."

We all had martinis and I proposed a toast to the new bride. Later, with a second martini, Tom raised his glass and proposed my mother's health.

Valerie said that they had been grandly entertained at the University of Texas. "They were so pleased to welcome Tom. He opened an exhibition of his first editions and papers."

Tom told us of the elaborate precautions taken to preserve the University collections. "Not only air conditioning, but moisture control—everything!"

Valerie added, "Tom is now an honorary sheriff—remind me to show you his badge when we return to Margie's!"

I thanked Tom for sending me a presentation copy of his Minneapolis lecture, *The Frontiers of Criticism,* and reminded him that we hadn't spoken of the event, adding, *"Time* magazine said that it was the largest number of persons ever assembled to hear a lecture on literary criticism, and the photograph they printed showed an immense stadium that was packed to the very top with fifteen thousand people!"

Tom cleared his throat and replied, "I had no idea that the audience was to be of that size, and I'm glad I didn't know because I wouldn't have had any idea what to say. You know, William, I do not believe there are fifteen thousand people in the entire world who are interested in criticism!"

Tom raised his eyebrows and smiled broadly when my mother brought in a cobalt-blue dish which he had admired on his last visit—containing black olives! He wasted no time in selecting one of the largest. As he devoured it and reached for another, he smiled at my mother appreciatively—and winked!

Tom said to me, "I am glad that you reviewed the Kenner book in *The Christian Scholar* [Hugh Kenner, *T. S. Eliot: The Invisible Poet*]. I agree with you that his chapter on F. H. Bradley contains the most valuable new information for the reader. I especially like the title of Kenner's book. I like the image; it's very appropriate."

Kenner had been the first to read Tom's doctoral dissertation on F. H. Bradley, the philosopher, and see in it Bradley's influence on Tom's early thought. The influence extended even to Tom's choice of words and the shaping of his unique prose style.

Tom normally made it a point not to comment on books written about his work. When I had asked him, some years earlier, however, what book he thought was the best among those written about his work, he answered without hesitation, "Helen Gardner's book" [*The Art of T. S. Eliot*]. "She has done a fine job, in my opinion."

I took a small book, in French, out of a glass bookcase, and passed it to Tom without comment.

He was startled to recognize that it was the first volume of his French edition of the works of St. Thomas Aquinas. "Did you get this from a bookseller?" he asked.

"Yes, I did," I replied, "with the intention of restoring it to you."

"Oh, no," he said, "this is yours now. I see it bears Gordon George's signature. How, I wonder, did it fall into his hands?" He looked at a few pages of the text and said, "The set has eleven or twelve volumes, and they are on my bookshelf at our apartment in Kensington Court Gardens."

Tom took out his fountain pen and inscribed the book to

me, below his own early signature and George's: "I don't know how this book came to have Gordon George's (i.e. 'Robert Sencourt') signature but it now belongs to my friend William Turner Levy. T. S. Eliot 27.iv.58."

I next showed Tom another new acquisition, two pages in Dylan Thomas's handwriting, from a notebook which he had used during his poetry readings. The pages contained the poem "Chard Witlow" by Henry Reed, a facetious take-off on Tom's "Burnt Norton." Tom gave it a close scrutiny, and remarked, "You know, I've been chairman of the British group that has been raising funds for Dylan Thomas's family. Caitlin, his wife, asked me to—a very sad business." Thomas's death in New York had left his family almost penniless.

Tom removed his fountain pen from his inside breast pocket and wrote on the bottom of the second of the two pages. When he finished, he handed it to my parents, who read it and passed it to Valerie. When it reached my hands, Tom said, "You know, William, this is the only piece of paper in existence that has both Dylan's writing on it and mine."

I read what he had written: "Not bad. But I think I could write a better parody myself! T. S. Eliot, 27.iv.58."

To be polite, I asked the Eliots if they would like another martini. I was thunderstruck when Tom immediately accepted the offer. We all had a third, ice-cold, bone-dry Beefeater martini.

Mother asked Tom, "Are you bothered a great deal by people who want to see you or question you about your work?"

Tom answered, "When I travel I am; for instance, once in Chicago, some time ago, a newspaper reporter bluntly asked me at the railroad station, 'What *was* the love life of J. Alfred Prufrock?' "

"And what did you tell him?" I asked.

"I told him, as I hastened on, I am afraid that was precisely Prufrock's trouble—he hadn't any!" Tom threw back his head and laughed.

Valerie said, "Tom, do tell the lion-tamer story!"

"Oh, it is too long to go into, dear," he replied modestly.

"Do tell it, Tom!" I requested.

"You may be sorry!" he said jokingly. He took a sip from his martini, clutched the lapels of his jacket with both hands, cleared his throat, and said, "I remember so well an old American vaudeville act—two men, Moran and Mack, who put on blackface and called themselves 'Two Black Crows.' This was their lion-tamer routine."

Tom recited the following in a well-rehearsed and professional manner. He had obviously performed the routine many times; his timing was perfect and his intonations embellished the thin material:

I'd like to train lions.

You know, to be a lion trainer, you gotta be very quick.

Well, I *am* quick.

How quick?

Oh, I'm so quick, when I go to bed at night, I turn out the light twenty feet from the bed, and I'm in bed before the room is dark.

Boy, when are you goin' to stop lyin'?

No, that's a fact, and all you got to do to train lions, you just throw salt on his tail and then you got him, or else—

Else what?

Else you're in a awful fix.

No, the first thing you do is you get up early in the morning and go down to the lion's cage and get a great big piece of raw meat.

Uh-huh.

You throw the raw meat into the lion's cage.

Oh-oh.

And then all you do, you open the door, jump inside the cage and take the raw meat away from the lion.

Oh, behave yourself, boy. You got lion taming mixed up with suicide.

And then all you do, you look the lion right straight in the eye and make him believe you're not afraid of him.

I—I couldn't be so deceitful. I couldn't do that. All I gotta do, like Daniel did in the lion's den, that's the way I like to train him.

I hope you don't believe all you heard about Daniel in the lions' den, do you?

I don't believe he swallowed the whale, I don't believe that, but I believe Daniel was in the lions' den and the wild lion never teched Daniel.

They weren't no wild, ferocious mountain lions; they were old circus lions.

Oh, man, this happened way back in B.C.

B what?

B.C.—Before Circuses.

Tom was uproarious in the telling, not only in repeating the patter, but also because the Negro dialect which he thought he had mastered made him sound more like an Archbishop of Canterbury!

Tom asked to use my bathroom and I anticipated what he would say upon his return. "William, that is a wonderful framed cat cartoon in your bathroom!"

I grinned and said, "It's yours! I hung it there temporarily to take you by surprise. It's a gift from me to you!"

I took it off the wall and brought it to Valerie, saying, "For your new home!"

It was an original strip cartoon by the well-known cartoonist of *The New Yorker,* Cobean, showing a cat frightened by a large and ferocious-looking dog; the cat, alone, imagining herself chasing the dog; and then later, frightened by the dog once again.

Valerie proudly showed my parents and me a gold charm bracelet which Tom had given her. It consisted of miniature books, each bearing the title of one of Tom's major works.

After dinner, Tom said to my mother, "Once again, Florence, your dinner was superb! I won't say anything more, however, because I dread after-dinner speeches."

Valerie added, "Tom says that speeches before a dinner are likely to ruin one's appetite, and if they come after the meal, they give one indigestion!"

Tom laughed, pleased that Valerie had remembered and repeated the quip. "The one thing that makes such speeches almost tolerable at stiff, formal dinners, is the relief they afford from talking to your neighbor!"

My parents and I drove the Eliots back to Margie Cohn's apartment, thus prolonging the pleasure of the visit.

Tom was giving a poetry reading at Columbia University the

following evening and had arranged for us to have tickets. "Be sure to come backstage afterwards," he encouraged. We did so, but stayed only briefly because of the crowd of people waiting to see him.

Before we left, Tom found a moment, however, to tell me privately, "I am very happy, William. This last part of my life is the best, in excess of anything I could have deserved."

# *Chapter Twelve*

One month after the Eliots were back in London, my father died. I received the following cablegram from Tom and Valerie, dated July 4, 1958: "We send our affectionate sympathy and pray for his repose."

Two days later, Tom wrote the following letter to my mother and me:

"Your cable arrived almost simultaneously with William's letter. The latter held out so little hope that we could hardly expect Jack to live much longer. He had had a long and distressing illness—he and both of you bore up under it nobly. Nevertheless, we grieve that he is gone; such a gentle, kindly man as he, must have been loved by many people. We think of you in your great loss and have mentioned him in our prayers. God bless you both."

On January 18, 1959, I was surprised to receive a telephone call from Tom, telling me that he and Valerie were in

New York, stopping briefly at Margie Cohn's en route to Nassau for a vacation. Upon his invitation, my mother and I went to a small bon-voyage gathering at their hostess's apartment.

In March, when they returned to New York from the Bahamas, Tom telephoned me once again.

"Valerie and I would like to take you and Florence to lunch. Are you free the day after tomorrow?"

"Yes, we are, but I insist that *we* take *you!*"

At the restaurant, over a Scotch and water before lunch, Tom told us that he was going to order all the food he couldn't get in England. He ordered pink grapefruit, shad and roe, eggplant and a chocolate éclair.

The éclair Tom ordered reminded me of a childhood experience I had had involving a chocolate ice cream cone. The ice cream had fallen out of the cone and onto the sidewalk after my first bite. I wailed. Almost at once, for we were still in front of the ice cream parlor, my mother bought me another. But, as I looked down at the ice cream melting on the hot concrete, I was inconsolable: the second ice cream cone couldn't make up for the loss of the first!

Tom said, "I had a similar experience, William, at the age of seven. I was very proud of a naval cap I had, bearing the insignia of crossed sabers from a Civil War uniform. I leaned out of the narrow aperture of a train window. The train started . . . I withdrew my head quickly . . . and the cap fell out the window. I cried and cried. It was, like yours, one of those losses that one suffers for a lifetime."

As usual, Tom asked in some detail about the courses I was teaching. When he heard that one of them included Dante, he questioned me about the text I was using. I told him that I had always been partial to the Carlyle-Okey-Wicksteed translation. Tom said, "I recommend the Binyon translation. Read it and see what you think."

I told him that his essay on Dante and Charles Williams's *The Figure of Beatrice* had encouraged me to read Dante.

"I am glad to have had a part in that," he said, "and I know the way you feel. I have always been grateful to Pound for insisting that I read Dante."

Tom told me that he was gratified that I was not teaching modern poetry. "I deplore the teaching of modern poets like myself. A good student will read contemporary poetry as naturally as he would read the newspapers. Besides, it is too early to know which of the moderns are worth considering!"

Enjoying a sip of Moselle, Tom spoke of his and Valerie's desire that we come to London to visit them. "I feel I owe you so much in the way of hospitality, and there is so much you would both enjoy in London."

My mother expressed her fear of the ocean and of flying. She said, "I'm hopeless. But, I'll be the first one over when they build a transatlantic tunnel!"

Tom was persistent: "Now, William, you must give Florence pills beforehand, to calm her; then you must highjack her aboard the plane; and then you must give her pills during the flight to combat airsickness!"

I looked skeptical, but he urged its implementation: "One does have to break down a person's resistance sometimes!"

As we emerged from the restaurant and put Tom and Valerie into a taxicab, Tom said, "I miss Wimsey. I promise to come again to see him in the fall." Taking our hands, he said,

"I miss Fairfield Avenue [our address in Riverdale], your things, your view."

I kissed Valerie, Tom kissed my mother, and he said, "God bless you both."

Some months later, my book on William Barnes was about to be published in England by Longmans (Dorchester) with an introduction by Mark Van Doren, who had encouraged me while I was writing it at Columbia. I asked Longmans to send an advance copy of the book to Tom. On June 18, 1959, Tom wrote me:

"I have just received from Longmans (Dorchester) Ltd. an advance bound proof of your William Barnes. They seem to me to have done a very good job with it, and I am rereading it with great pleasure. I think you have done a very good job too, and I do hope the book will have a good sale. Your typescript, you will remember, was my introduction to this poet and I know that your quotations ought to do a great deal to gain him further, greater recognition."

Longmans was good enough to send me Tom's letter to them of the same date. It read:

"I thank you for sending me the proof copy of the excellent book on William Barnes by The Rev. William Turner Levy. I congratulate you on publishing this book and on the format and typography. I do hope that it will be well received and have a good sale."

Both Tom and Valerie wrote individually to tell me that they were sailing for New York on October 8, and on their arrival would proceed immediately to St. Louis by way of Chicago. They would then travel to Cambridge and hope to see us afterwards in New York before they sailed back to England.

We arranged to attend All Angels' Church and have Sunday dinner at my home on November 15. At the service, I preached on Samuel Johnson, churchman and man of letters, as a compliment to Tom, whom I considered a similar figure. In the course of the sermon I alluded to the example of Johnson's life, to the magnificent prayers he composed, and to the extraordinary faith and patience with which he endured his final months of pain. I concluded:

"Here then is Samuel Johnson, an ordinary man, but *Christianus,* of Christ; no saint, but a man who triumphed in his life because he trusted and heeded his Lord.

"Surely one of the things we mean when we say, 'the communication of the dead is tongued with fire beyond the language of the living' [a quote from Eliot's "Little Gidding"], is that a man may, from the state we call death, help and strengthen us: pray the example of Samuel Johnson may work in you."

Wimsey was waiting for us at the door. Tom said, "Isn't it nice not to have to return to an empty house, but to have the privilege of a cat waiting for one!"

I told Tom that Una Jeffers (Mrs. Robinson Jeffers) eagerly asked me once if it were true, as Osbert Sitwell wrote in *Laughter in the Next Room,* that Eliot had the eyes and face of "one of the greater cats."

"Do you think you look like a cat?" I asked.

"I hope so, William. I hope so. That would be very pleasant to believe!"

Wimsey was overjoyed during cocktails, when Tom fed him innumerable shrimp from among those my mother had prepared for hors d'oeuvres.

"Once again, William, I would like to tell you how admirable I thought that sermon," Tom said. "I dare say it is the best one I have heard in the last three years." He reached over to my desk and picked up my notes on the sermon and was surprised to discover that except for a few salient paragraphs, I had not written it out. "I do not see how you can do it," Tom remarked, shaking his head in wonder; "it would be impossible for me. I have always written out and then read my lectures, even the sermon I delivered at Magdalene College."

Tom fed Wimsey another shrimp and then ate one himself. Both cat and poet chewed and swallowed at the same time. Tom said, looking at me over his glasses, "I agreed with your choice this morning. That is, to speak on some of the revealing episodes in Dr. Johnson's life."

In the sermon, I had retold the story of Johnson returning, in the last year of his life, to the city square where his father had had a bookstall and standing bareheaded in the rain for an hour as an act of penance for having disobeyed his father at that very spot exactly fifty years before. Tom remarked: "It may have done his father no good, at that time, but I have nothing but admiration for a man who can act in that way. It is a mark of his sensitivity and of the nicety with which he evaluated the obligation of duty."

I had also recounted that Dr. Johnson, even in weakness and great illness, went out to the fishmonger to buy food for his cat Hodge, so that a servant might not be unkind to the animal because it caused extra work. "I have always found that very touching," Tom said, "and it contains, alas, a just estimation of human nature."

As I poured our second martini, Tom said to my mother, "I'm afraid I'm encouraging Wimsey in extravagant tastes, Florence! I know that when Pettipaws was on his Belgian hare diet it cost us seven shillings sixpence a week!" Wimsey's only reaction was to remind Tom, by reaching out with his paw and tapping Tom's knee, that he wanted at least one more shrimp.

At dinner, Tom asked if he might propose the toast. Standing and raising his wine glass, he said, "To the immortal memory of Samuel Johnson!"

We had coffee in my study after dinner. Tom, seated on the sofa once again, lit a cigar, smiled in contentment and said, "A self-indulgence which I only allow myself on special occasions."

Tom dropped several cubes of sugar into his coffee, stirred it gently for a long time and asked, "Did I ever tell you the story about Gladstone and Queen Victoria?"

"No, you haven't," I replied, moving my chair closer.

Wimsey entered the room and took his customary place on a cushioned chair in the corner. He settled himself and then looked at Tom expectantly. Tom chuckled and said, "Now that we're *all* here, I can tell the story! It seems that Gladstone was present at a soiree given by the Queen. Directly after the banquet, the gentlemen went to the smoking room and a butler passed cigars on a silver tray. Noticing that Gladstone did not take one, a gentleman inquired if he did not smoke. Gladstone replied casually, 'Rarely, rarely . . . only on special occasions!' "

Tom always seemed to me the least likely person to tell a funny story. When he did tell a joke or anecdote, however, he was uncommonly successful. He would lose himself completely in dramatizing the story, enjoying it as though he were hearing it himself for the first time.

With a cup of coffee in his hand, Tom walked over to a small hanging bookcase with glass doors that he knew had been made for Franklin Delano Roosevelt, and that contained about forty volumes of miniature books which had been part of the President's collection. There had never, on previous visits, been enough time for me to show them to him. Now, he peered through the glass and asked if he might see a few.

Tom was particularly interested in some early English chapbooks, containing the original printings of nursery rhymes like "Ride a cock horse to Banbury Cross" and "This is the house that Jack built." Two pieces of historic interest fascinated him. One was a set of four volumes of French plays which came out of the library of Chancellor Robert Livingston, who had administered the oath of office to George Washington, financed Robert Fulton's *Clermont,* and was the prime mover in the Louisiana Purchase. Picking up Livingston's calling card, which he had used as a bookmark in one of the volumes, Tom showed it to Valerie. It bore an engraving of a rifle, and the motto, "Useful to him who knows how to use it" in Latin. The other book which Tom lingered over was a German yearbook of 1785, printing the American flag for the first time in color.

"I had no idea, William," Tom said, "that Roosevelt was such a discriminating collector. This is an historic collection, especially with the President's signature and date in each volume."

Curiously enough, no reference was made to the plate.

I presented the Eliots with a copy of the William Barnes book, which I had had especially bound for them by Sangorski and Sutcliffe in London. Then, speaking of books, I said that I had been impressed with *The Mint* by T. E. Lawrence—which had after all these years been published for the first time—and considered it the best book ever written about army life in the barracks. I read aloud a short passage to give an idea of its quality, and Tom said, "I have not read it. As far as I know, it did not attract much notice, certainly nothing as favorable as you indicate it deserves." He looked at the book and added: "I see this is the limited edition, which has not been expurgated. I will remember to read it on your recommendation."

As we continued to talk of war books, including C. E. Montague's *Disenchantment,* which we had both read and about which we had certain reservations, despite an appreciation of the value of its impact in its day, Tom asked me if I knew *Her Privates We,* which was written anonymously. When I said I had never even heard of it, he said, "You should read it. I think it the best book to have come out of the First World War. It communicates the 'feel' of trench warfare, which was the particular experience of the World War One soldier. The author had lived through it himself and decided to publish the book anonymously, only using his military serial number, in order to make it clear that he was writing as a representative of the enlisted man and not as an individual or from an officer's viewpoint."

When we bade the Eliots good-by, Tom said, "It has been a good year—we have had the opportunity to get over and see you *twice!* I have greatly enjoyed these trips to America. It is a privilege to live, in a sense, in two cultures, and I am grateful for it. Each is more interesting because of the contrast with the other. I believe I have the best of both possible worlds!" Thoughtfully, Tom concluded, "In some ways I am very American; yes, ah . . . and in some ways"—he glanced down at his umbrella and smiled—"very British!"

His parting sally was, "Well—good-by, ah . . . or—cheerio!"

[*119*]

## Chapter Thirteen

The Church of the Transfiguration in New York City is better known as "The Little Church Around the Corner." It is closely associated with actors, particularly Episcopal actors, because at a time early in New York's history, when the profession was snubbed by other churches, this attractive, English-style countrylike church welcomed actors. Tom had spoken of it, remembered reading of many famous theatrical weddings and funerals that had taken place within its walls, and asked to go there some Sunday.

On March 12, 1961, together with my mother and Valerie, Tom and I attended the Choral Eucharist at eleven in the morning. The Very Reverend Lawrence Rose, then Dean of General Theological Seminary, was the preacher. There was a motet and organ fantasia, both by Orlando Gibbons, and Tom and I, for the only time, received the Sacrament together.

As we left the church on that mid-Lent Sunday, Tom told

me that the Church had defined good and evil for him, whereas, as a child, "All that concerned my family was 'right and wrong,' what was 'done and not done.'" We walked silently behind the ladies for a few minutes and then Tom concluded his thought: "It is necessary to realize that every act of ours results in positive good or positive evil. There's no escape from that!"

As we reached the car, parked just a block away, Tom said, "I see you have a handsome new automobile, William," adding, as he stepped in, "All motors are a mystery to me, outside my experience."

On the drive to Fairfield Avenue for Sunday dinner, we all spoke of beautiful church buildings, and I mentioned that Notre Dame de la Gard, high up overlooking the Mediterranean at Marseilles, was one of the churches I had found most impressive. It is hung with ship models and is a church for men who go down to the sea in ships. Tom intoned, "Lady, whose shrine stands on the promontory," the first line from the fourth part of "The Dry Salvages," and then said, "Notre Dame de la Gard is the church I had in mind when I wrote that line."

I couldn't believe my own failure to have realized this, but Tom said, "You accepted it as a class of churches, and were not thinking of a particular church. And that is the right way to think of it. It is fortuitous in our case that I as writer and you as reader of these lines happened to know and react identically to the same place—and then we had to know each other for me to affirm it!"

Tom and Valerie commented on the splendid music in the service that morning, Tom saying that on his last trip to

Munich he had attended a festival service in a church with the most beautiful string quartet he had ever heard. "The acoustics of the building, no doubt," he said, "and the age of the wood in the stalls and pews all contributed to the purity of tone."

Not until we were in the elevator going up to the apartment did I realize that Tom was wearing the necktie I had given him on his birthday two years ago. He saw that I had noticed it and said, touching it with his hand, "Elegant."

Tom knew that Wimsey would be at the door.

"Ah . . . Lord Peter Wimsey, it's your Uncle Tom Possum!" Wimsey reacted by rolling on his back and leaping to a chair. Tom said, "You're very acrobatic . . . but are you a practical cat?"

Tom walked into the living room and noticed our television set for the first time; it was a portable model with an eight-inch screen.

"William, that is the smallest television set I have ever seen!"

"You know, Tom, my students ask if it's Wimsey's!"

Tom enjoyed a good laugh.

Speaking of television, Tom commented: "I prefer live entertainment—except for a few fine film actors—and regret the passing of the old music halls. Marie Lloyd, I recall, was a real artist. Her audiences would join in the choruses of her numbers. In all genuine art there is the necessary collaboration of audience and artist."

We had Stilton cheese and smoked salmon with our martinis.

I showed Tom and Valerie the manuscript of Robinson

Jeffers's poem "Oh, Lovely Rock." Jeffers, a friend, had sent it to me the year before. I thought the Eliots would be interested in the three or four false starts on paper before Jeffers arrived at the final version. An individual word would be crossed out again and again in the search for the right word. Tom put on his glasses and questioned me about some of the handwriting that was hard to decipher. I gave him a printed copy of the final poem to put alongside it. As I expected, Tom was engrossed with the revisions. "This is an extraordinary view into the creative process," he commented. "I don't work this way. I usually end up with a single clean copy, each of the other copies having been a retyping of the previous one, which had been thrown away. I can see this would be of real interest to scholars."

Observing a Ronald Searle drawing on the wall, Valerie asked me if I had seen the caricature he had done of Tom for *Punch*. I said I had but didn't like it. Tom said, "It seems to me not to capture anything, not to amuse, not to serve any recognizable purpose—however, I generally admire his work."

I took the Searle drawing off the wall so that they could examine it more closely. It was a drawing of great power, the subject—an aged refugee woman. Tom was struck by Searle's "unsentimental compassion."

Because I knew he loved Edward Lear's nonsense verse and owned a Lear watercolor himself, I showed Tom an impressionistic Lear watercolor of a Greek olive grove with the sea in the distance. It had never seemed more beautiful to me than at that moment, when, in a perfect light, Tom admired it.

Next, I took down a watercolor illustration from *David Copperfield* by Hablot K. Browne ("Phiz"). It showed the parson preaching away and all the congregation distracted or asleep. It was complete with a church mouse and a bat from the belfry. Tom looked at the congregation a second time and said seriously, "That would never happen if William were preaching!"

Finally, his eye was caught by an imaginative watercolor by the Reverend William Gilpin of a fantastically large umbrella-like mushroom, under which were gathered a conversing group of philosophers. "Now that is truly Utopia," Tom said; "that fellow had the right idea!"

After dinner, I played for the Eliots a dryly amusing story recorded by Eleanor Roosevelt. It was written by Belle (Mrs. Kermit) Roosevelt and was called "The Sprout Incident." It related how F.D.R. told Lady Churchill that he was appalled by the way the English cooked Brussels sprouts, boiling them to death and serving them in tepid water. When Lady Churchill replied, "Not boil Brussels sprouts?" F.D.R. was carried away and launched out on a tale of America's favorite dish—*broiled* Brussels sprouts. The President's joke had later repercussions for the American ambassador in London, and confused diplomatic relations!

I had hoped that Tom and Valerie would be amused, despite the dig at England's only vegetable! Tom said—and I thought it a perfect comment, equally applicable to his own storytelling—"Mrs. Roosevelt is a superb storyteller. Her sense of fun is infectious—her timing and the way she uses her voice is perfect!"

Tom knew that beginning in 1955 I had designed an original Christmas card each year and had used quotations from the published work of friends. The list of contributors had included Mark Van Doren, Padraic Colum, Adlai Stevenson, Reinhold Niebuhr, Eleanor Roosevelt and Robinson Jeffers.

Over coffee and a white creme de menthe, I told Tom that I had a favor to ask of him, which he was perfectly free to refuse. "I'd like to use a line from the *Four Quartets* this year on my Christmas card," I said, "in your handwriting."

Tom asked immediately, "Which line, William?"

" 'Prayer, observance, discipline, thought and action,' " I replied. "I plan to do a simple drawing, as usual, on page one, saying 'Merry Christmas and a Happy New Year from William Turner Levy,' in my handwriting; then on page two, 'The rest is,' and on page three, your line. The back of the folder will say, if you agree, 'Five words in his own hand by T. S. Eliot.' "

Tom seemed very pleased. "I think it a very appropriate card for Christmas. Very. Is there a special piece of paper you want me to write them on?"

He wrote out the words, one under the other, on my personal writing paper, and at the bottom of the sheet added, "5 words written out for W.T.L. by T. S. Eliot," circled it and carried the line up to my own name at the top of the sheet and circled that!

The card was much admired.

Tom's Christmas cards over the years were always those made for the directors of Faber & Faber. They were the most original, colorful and beautiful I have ever seen, each having been designed by outstanding contemporary artists, such as John Piper and David Jones.

Tom and Valerie came to America again in November. Tom lectured and read at the Y.M.H.A. in New York, lectured at

Yale and, while staying with his family in Cambridge, gave readings at Boston College and the Massachusetts Institute of Technology.

My mother and I saw them in New York on January 2, 1962, before they sailed for Barbados for a two-month holiday.

Valerie had told me on the telephone beforehand that Tom was exhausted and that to conserve his energy it would be better just to have a drink and a light lunch together at the River Club, where they were staying.

Mother and I were in the empty drawing room of the River Club when I heard the elevator doors open. I hastened to see if it were the Eliots. It was. Tom was bent over and walking very slowly with the aid of a cane. His physiognomy was altered; not only was he an ashen color, but the very features themselves seemed softened and flabby. His voice was weak when he slowly raised his cane to emphasize his greeting. I was shocked.

Valerie ordered drinks and sat next to my mother on a sofa, while Tom, who had difficulty lowering himself into a gold, upholstered chair, sat next to me.

I spoke to him gently, as one does to the infirm.

He began by telling me that he had heard a wonderfully useful story. It concerned the Scottish theologian-clergyman John Baillie, whom Tom knew I admired. "Like yours, his duties and responsibilities were onerous. He began to find that he hadn't the necessary time to meditate, to think out and write his sermons. So he hit upon an idea. He named his upstairs study, 'Edinburgh,' a city some thirty or forty miles distant. One day a week, he didn't leave his room; his housekeeper brought up his meals; he had a day to read and write. Whenever the doorbell rang, or the telephone, his housekeeper could honestly reply, 'I'm sorry, but the parson is in Edinburgh!'"

Tom told me, "I have just done an introduction to a collection of George Herbert's poems, and Faber is bringing out my doctoral thesis on F. H. Bradley. I read the Bradley book over carefully, and wrote an introduction. I found that I could not understand the thesis and said so—it is so many years since I have thought in philosophic categories! I suppose it is being published as a sort of curiosity!"

Tom looked over to my mother, and told her how well she looked.

After a few pleasantries, he asked me if I had read *The New English Bible*. When I said I hadn't he said, "I think you will be dismayed by it, as I am, William. Not just stylistic losses, nuances gone, language forced, but, for example, instead of being admonished not to cast pearls before swine, we are now instructed, 'Do not feed your pearls to pigs'—and so the meaning is quite simply destroyed!"

Tom occasionally took a swallow of his drink, but without relish.

I said, "You know, Tom, I've often wondered why you wrote the book on Ezra Pound anonymously [*Ezra Pound, His Metric and Poetry,* 1917]."

"Because I was a very young man then, just starting my writing career, and it would have been presumptuous of me to offer my opinions except on their own merits."

He looked up with a touch of animation. "Any more questions, William?"

[*127*]

"Well, I've always meant to ask you if the Order of Merit [Britain's highest nonmilitary honor—limited to twenty-four living persons] is like a medal. Is it worn about the neck?"

"Yes. It is a rather large, enameled, beautiful work—in the general shape of a Maltese cross. Of course, I wear it only on very rare ceremonial occasions. It was presented to me by the King in a very simple way in a very short audience. I will show it to you when you come to England."

Tom asked me what I was doing. I told him briefly what I thought was worth his attention, adding that I had been invited by General William C. Westmoreland, then Commandant of the United States Military Academy at West Point, whom I had twice lunched with at Mrs. Roosevelt's in Hyde Park, to deliver a lecture to the cadets on someone called T. S. Eliot! Tom was impressed. "You will have to give me a full report on *that,* William. I shall be most interested to know what you said."

He lapsed into silence for a moment, then said, "And when you find time, you should develop 'The Idea of the Church in T. S. Eliot' into a longer study. If you need to know any facts, I can always supply them."

I asked him a final question: "I think I understand what these lines from 'Little Gidding' mean, but I'd like to hear what you have to say about them." I recited the lines:

*"And what the dead had no speech for, when living,*
*They can tell you, being dead: the communication*
*Of the dead is tongued with fire beyond the language of the living."*

Tom replied, "I had chiefly in mind that we cannot fully understand a person, grasp the totality of his being, until he is dead. Once he is dead, the acts of his life fall into their proper perspective and we can see what he was tending toward. Also, with the living presence removed, it is easier to make an impartial judgment, free of the personality of the individual."

After lunch, Tom and Valerie walked my mother and me to the cloakroom and, with infinite courtesy, waited while we were given our coats.

"Thank you for coming," he said. "We shall have a longer time together on the next trip."

As I looked back for a last glimpse of Tom, I saw that he was leaning on Valerie's arm, wearily entering the elevator.

Out on the street I turned to my mother and said, "I wonder if we will ever see Tom again."

I was saddened, and that night I dreamed of flying to Tom's sickbed in London.

# Chapter Fourteen

Eight days later, on their fifth wedding anniversary, the Eliots were aboard ship, bound for Barbados in the British West Indies. I cabled them that Mother and I would lift our glasses to them that evening at dinner.

I received an air-mail postcard in Tom's hand: "We very much appreciated your message on our anniversary. Your memory never fails! This is the third time we have had to celebrate it at sea. We were sorry to hear of Jeffers' death and thought of you too. We swim every morning, and I am already very brown. Love to both of you from T. & V."

The following month, to relieve my anxiety, I telephoned Tom in Barbados. He, Valerie, Mother and I had a good talk. His description of St. James, the sun, the shoreline, the ocean, the trees, was a verbal picture of the postcard scene he had sent. "I'm sleeping late, William, and eating very well. I get in the water, and I'm getting very tan!" It was all very reassuring.

Back in London, Tom wrote and thanked me for the latest Pogo book which I had sent him:

"I liked the last one because I was glad to see some of my old friends such as Bun Rabbit and Albert the Alligator. Personally I thought that Walt Kelly had become rather tiresome with his snakes, worms and insects who haven't the same warmth of appeal as the rabbit, the tortoise and the alligator, to say nothing of Pogo himself."

I wrote a tribute to Robinson Jeffers in the "Speaking of Books" column in *The New York Times Book Review,* and Tom commented: "I like your piece about Robinson Jeffers. It is curious that he seems to have had less adulation than some other poets whom I find less interesting. Jeffers and Conrad Aiken have never been adequately appreciated, nor for that matter is my friend Djuna Barnes."

Tom suffered a serious illness and was not able to come to America for Christmas in 1962. My mother and I sent flowers and notes, and then on February 11, 1963, Valerie wrote:

"The four-day smog early in December proved too much for Tom's heart and lungs and he collapsed critically ill. He spent five weeks in the Brompton Hospital—perhaps England's finest hospital for chest and lung complaints—under continuous oxygen. By the Grace of God and his own determination (medically everything seemed hopeless) he pulled through. We were touched, as always, by your remembrance of our wedding anniversary and he kept your card by him.

"Just over three weeks ago I brought him home, as excited as a schoolboy after his first term away. As he has to make no exertion I wash and shave him and see that he swallows 26 pills a day. He has put on half a stone, looks a better colour, is very serene and grows daily more mischievous—the latter being an excellent sign.

"We have no plans at present. He still has a long slow way to go. I see daily improvements, however, and he is helping himself in every respect. His pulse is steadier but his lungs will always be a problem as he suffers from emphysema. He is eating and sleeping well."

I received the following letter, dated October 12, 1963, from Tom. It was the last letter I would receive signed in his own hand.

"My very grateful thanks for the delightful scarf you sent me. It really is quite lovely and I shall be very proud to wear it.

"We shall hope to have a glimpse of you in New York, though we cannot undertake to go out to have a meal with you and Florence on this occasion. I must be very quiet while there and make no public engagements whatever. I shall just see a few people, and perhaps you could look in at the River Club while we are staying there. We shall then go on to Nassau for two months if there is anything left of it after the hurricane."

My mother and I saw Tom for the last time on December 23, 1963, at the River Club.

# *Chapter Fifteen*

A few days before our last meeting, I bought an outsize crystal brandy glass, filled it with several dozen small brightly colored Christmas tree ornaments and delivered it to the River Club. The switchboard operator behind the desk told me that it would be sent up to the Eliots' room immediately.

That evening Valerie telephoned, "We love our gay Christmas decoration, William! It was sweet of you and Florence to think of it. Thank you so much! Tom is resting now, but we'd both love to have you and Florence come to us for cocktails and dinner. Tom assumed that you would have an evening Mass on Christmas Eve, so could you both come on the twenty-third instead, at seven?"

When I said how happy we would be to dine with them, Valerie replied, "Good. We'll have a table reserved in our name in the cocktail room! It will be so nice to see you both!"

It began to snow in the early afternoon of the twenty-third, and the accumulation was alarming. The radio carried dire reports hourly and New York became disrupted and paralyzed. My mother was nervous about the drive downtown, but nothing would have prevented me from going. When a blizzard comes, I prefer to be the driver, and so I vetoed her suggestion of a hired car. I had to admit to myself, however, that the risk was great and that we might end up in a snowdrift, but I was determined that we'd start. Dressed against the weather, we left the house at five-thirty, having first taken the precaution of calling a garage across the street from the River Club and getting them to revise their rules to let us in. At five minutes to seven precisely, we made the hazardous walk across the blustery street to the back, or delivery, entrance of the River Club.

At seven o'clock we entered the cocktail lounge just two minutes before the Eliots. Tom, I recognized with a sinking feeling, looked, if anything, worse than the last time we saw him. He moved into the room with great effort and somehow his large frame, so stooped, made his condition visibly undeniable.

After we had greeted each other, Tom, who was suffering great shortness of breath, said, "I knew you would be here, William, and on time!" Valerie said that we deserved some special sort of medal.

The club was very quiet and private that night.

Valerie said she was happy to see us so fit. My voice on the telephone, apparently, had sounded very serious.

"Were you calling from the church, William?" Tom asked.

"No, from home."

"No excuse, then," he countered; "I was going to say it was

your 'vestry voice.'" He attempted a weak little laugh, which turned into a cough.

Tom ordered drinks, deciding upon a daiquiri for himself. When we had our drinks and had clinked our glasses together, Tom said, "I hope the martini is good. You make yours with such pharmaceutical perfection!"

The Eliots had been traveling, and I learned from Valerie that catching a train was a traumatic experience for Tom. "Yes," Tom volunteered, "when I was a boy and we traveled by train from St. Louis to the East, I was always apprehensive. I always feared that it would pull out in front of our eyes, or that my father, busy with seeing the luggage put aboard, would miss the train. I found a variety of calamities to worry about. And I haven't changed!"

I asked Tom if he often thought of his childhood.

"More often lately, William. I had a dream the other night of my family as it was at that time. Curious. And I was thinking the other day of how as a child I never got anything new, always hand-me-downs from my brother. I remember a toby-dog my mother made for my brother and when he had outgrown any interest in it, it was given to me! And my favorite childhood toy was a rocking horse—with real skin. It was a very expensive one, but somehow my mother got it cheaply—for my brother. By the time I got it, there were cracks in the skin."

Valerie said it was time for our presents. I had noticed the two beautifully wrapped Christmas boxes in red paper with green ribbon, but didn't know they were for us. We had sent their gifts to London, not realizing that they would be in America over the holidays.

Tom brightened as he helped Valerie with the presentation. He said, "We hope Florence will like this!" She did. It was a box of assorted Elizabeth Arden toiletries. "And this is something for William. Something *I* like!" It was a bottle of Bristol Cream sherry. "And," he concluded, smiling at Valerie, "our third present is for both of you—you will be receiving a subscription to *The Illustrated London News* with our love!"

Tom seemed bone tired. He ordered another round of drinks and we chatted quietly.

It was nine o'clock when we entered the dining room. The dinner was excellent and Tom ordered a 1949 Hermitage to go with our roast beef. I was touched when Tom, who apparently could not eat them any longer himself, urged me to have oysters. I did, and as I was enjoying them, he looked at me and said, "I love to see people eat oysters!"

He ate sparingly himself and, for that reason, took a special delight in my full appreciation of each course. "I love vichyssoise," I told him. "Good, good!" he replied smiling happily.

We lingered over our wine, and Tom looked much better. He talked with a stronger voice and took a more active part in the exchanges.

"I am so pleased you sent me *Parade's End* for my birthday," he said. "I have not yet read it, but it is high on my list of books to read. Are you familiar with his novel *Ladies Whose Bright Eyes?*"

"No," I replied, "the only novels of Ford Madox Ford I've read are *Parade's End* and *The Good Soldier.*"

"Then you have a treat in store. I am so glad that you have the pleasure of reading it before you. If you encounter any difficulty procuring a copy, let me know."

I told him that I would, and that I would think of him when I read it.

"Do that," he said. "I know you will like it."

To please Tom, as well as myself, I had both mince pie and pumpkin pie for dessert. Tom was eager to know which I thought superior as he ate his caramel custard.

It was ten-thirty when we finished dinner. Much to my delight, Tom suggested that we return to the cocktail lounge for an after-dinner drink. He was looking and feeling much better.

A warm Christmas spirit prevailed, and we maintained a conspiracy of silence about the weather outside. Once, we all looked otherwise preoccupied when we heard one waiter say to another that it was still snowing.

Tom said that he had seen an advertisement in *The* (London) *Times Literary Supplement* for my book on Barnes. "You did a fine service there!" Tom congratulated me. "I trust it is selling."

"Yes, it is," I answered. "I asked the publisher if perhaps he ought to insert another advertisement and he wrote me that it wouldn't be necessary, that it was holding up very well, selling a steady *two copies* a month!"

I admired Tom's multicolored but conservative necktie, and he said with a grin, "You know, someone told me once that I didn't dress like a poet! I suppose it is because I have always felt much too Bohemian inside to want to register it on the outside!"

"By the way," he asked me, alluding to our custom, "what have you brought for me to sign?"

I proudly produced his exceedingly rare poem *A Practical Possum,* privately printed at Harvard. He was delighted to sign it "T. S. Eliot (Possum himself)."

As he was signing it, I told Valerie that Tom had always been so very good to me, seeing me, upon occasion, when he saw no one else. Tom looked up, replaced his pen in his pocket, took off his glasses and, as he polished them with his breast-pocket handkerchief, said, "Well, one makes one's choices, doesn't one, and I have never regretted that one."

Tom ordered us another round of drinks—"It's Christmas, you know!"—then turning very serious, said to me, "You must miss Mrs. Roosevelt very much." (Eleanor Roosevelt had died November 7, 1962.)

"More and more," I said.

"I am so glad that you were asked to take her funeral," Tom said and then, abruptly changing the subject, asked, "Tell us about the West Point lecture!"

I told them that General and Mrs. Westmoreland's hospitality had been overwhelming. A magnificent dinner had been given in my honor in the early 19th-century house of the Commandant. The clock in the simple, elegant dining room had been a gift from Lafayette. The signature just before mine in the guest book was William Faulkner's. I told them, "You can't imagine any setting more beautiful. In the garden outside were towering trees, including magnolia."

Then I told Tom that I had taken it as my responsibility to tell these men in one hour the essence of his work. What is he saying to us? "I showed that you were concerned with unmasking the person, with tearing down the façade we each more or less successfully construct to protect ourselves from others and from ourselves. I explained that we do not live until we have the courage to face reality. I used your lines that, if you haven't the strength to impose your own terms upon life, then life would impose its terms upon you. I told them that you were saying two things, first, that love cannot grow between persons who are insulated from each other and not willing to be vulnerable; and second, that God can speak to the *real* person only and is irrelevant to our masked, façaded self."

Tom hunched forward, his big hands upon his knees. "You feel that I have been saying this from the *very* beginning?"

"I do. Not that you knew it, but even in early poems like 'Spleen' and 'Aunt Helen' you were showing the façade that had been erected."

Tom said, "This is very convincing, and I would like to think that it is true."

I said, "The cadets were impressed to discover how meaningful poetry can be. Their questions afterward were all related to the risks involved in facing life without a mask, but the necessity to do so in order to achieve happiness."

Tom said, "Well, William, you certainly represented me better than I could have represented myself."

I added, quietly, "Tom . . . after the lecture, when I was having a drink with General Westmoreland, he paid *you,* not *me,* a supreme compliment. He told me that he had never before seen the Corps held in such rapt attention, although many illustrious writers, diplomats and statesmen had spoken to them. It was not my presentation, of course, but the significance of *your work* that arrested them."

Tom looked at me intently for a long moment. No one spoke, and then, with a sigh, he leaned back into his chair without comment.

Valerie said to Mother and me, "The Christmas decoration

you gave us is so special, and it really cheers our rooms. I know you intended us to have it only while staying here at the club, but we can't bear to leave it behind, and it would be too awkward to take with us on our travels. May I pack it up in the box it came in and leave it for you to pick up? Then, next Christmas you can give it to us again! We'd love that!"

Mother and I were flattered that they valued the Christmas decoration to that extent. We told them that we would be happy to keep it for them.

Before we departed, Tom happened to mention how much he admired Groucho Marx. I didn't find it surprising that Tom, who loved nonsense verse and inspired nonsense of any kind (including practical jokes), should have a high regard for Groucho Marx. Tom told me, "He is a master of nonsense. I love him! I never miss an opportunity to see one of his films when it is playing in London." Tom particularly relished the hilarity of *A Night at the Opera*. He told me that he corresponded with Marx, having written him a fan letter to begin with, and then they agreed to exchange photographs. The first photograph Groucho sent Tom showed him without the famous cigar. Tom lamented this absence when he wrote to thank Groucho, who then sent him a second photograph to put the matter right. The originality and quickness of Groucho's mind was awesome to Tom. "It is beyond me how he does it," he said, shaking his head with incredulity; "he is a comic genius, a very rare thing." I was led to ask about the other Marx Brothers. He thought for a moment, then replied judiciously: "One thinks of them, of course, as a unit, but when I see Groucho alone, I never miss the others."

At this moment of levity, I told Tom how useful I had

found two cartoons by Whitney Darrow, Jr., as illustrations in teaching. Both had appeared some years ago in *The New Yorker,* I said.

"In the first, we see a beautiful girl and a handsome boy on a mountain top. The sun is out, clouds scud by, birds are singing and they have a wonderful-looking picnic meal unpacked on the blanket. It's a *halcyon* day," I emphasized, and Tom acknowledged his adjective, used so effectively in *Four Quartets*. "Suddenly there is a frown on the young man's face —and it is clear that all is shattered. He says, 'Damn it, I forgot the cigarettes!' "

Tom was immensely amused.

"In the second cartoon, we are in, say, Rocky Mountain National Park. The scenery is spectacular beyond belief; on the road far below is a parked car and the minuscule forms of a man and a woman. She says to him, 'Doesn't it make you realize how insignificant *you* are!' "

Tom laughed and said, "They are very fine. I must remember them . . . 'how insignificant *you* are' . . . ah, *very* good."

Tom seemed to be consciously impressing this on his memory. Then he said, "I have remembered one cartoon from *The New Yorker*, too! We are in a cathedral, or very large church, and the organist is practicing at an enormous instrument with tiers upon tiers of organ pipes. There are two ladies in the foreground and one whispers to the other, 'He can imitate a mouse!' "

I told Tom that it would be my third remembered cartoon.

It was midnight and time to leave.

[*141*]

Tom and Valerie escorted us to the cloakroom. As they helped us into our coats, someone entered by the front door and we saw that the snow was still falling.

Tom furrowed his brow and said, "I worry about you. You must call us when you get home."

I protested, "It will be too late, Tom, it will take us an hour at least and you will want to get to bed."

Tom was adamant: "No, no, you *must* call us. I won't be able to sleep unless I know you arrived home safely."

Tom kissed my mother, I kissed Valerie, then Tom shook my hand, and said, "God bless you. Let us keep each other in our prayers until we see each other again."

# Chapter Sixteen

Tom wrote my mother and me his last letter on October 2, 1964. It read:

"It was very kind indeed of you to send me a telegram of greetings for my birthday. It gave me real pleasure."

In place of the usual signature, the following appeared at the bottom of the letter:

*"(Dictated by Mr. Eliot and*
*signed in his absence)"*

My friend T. S. Eliot died on January 4, 1965.

I telephoned Valerie as soon as I heard the news. She told me that he had died peacefully.

Incongruous irrelevancies somehow always seem to enter into life's gravest moments. I had a bit of trouble reaching Valerie despite having their private telephone number. Through the echoing and beeping quality of a transatlantic call, I heard an exchange I was not intended to hear between two male telephone operators:

"Valerie Eliot?"

"You know, that's the widow of the bloke that died yesterday."

There was nothing disrespectful in their tone, merely an acknowledgment that many calls were being received. Because it involved a fame they did not understand, T. S. Eliot retained a privacy that I imagine he would have accepted with gratitude.

# Index

[*145*]